I0148889

Advance Praise for One Simple Breath

"Patty manages to do the seemingly impossible task of offering caregivers a way to care for themselves while caring for others. She accomplishes this by giving words to the act of breathing itself, enlivening the breath with intention and feeling.

Although written for caregivers, One Simple Breath is a book for anyone seeking to be more mindful, honest, and compassionate in each moment. I felt engulfed in peaceful space as I continued to read and give voice to my breath."

-DEBORAH ADELE
Author of *The Yamas & Niyamas: Exploring Yoga's Ethical Practice*

"Patty Collamer's *One Simple Breath: A Caregiver's Guide to Inner Peace* is a truly compassionate gift to anyone in a caregiving role. Collamer offers a realistic and entirely helpful set of necessary suggestions allowing us to care for others while also caring for ourselves."

~DINTY W. MOORE
Author of *The Mindful Writer*

One Simple Breath

A Caregiver's Guide to
Inner Peace

Patty Collamer

Year of the Book
135 Glen Avenue
Glen Rock, PA 17327

Copyright © 2021 Patty Collamer
All Rights Reserved

No part of this publication may be reproduced, distributed, or transmitted in any form or by any means, including photocopying, recording, or other electronic or mechanical methods, without the prior written permission of the publisher, except in the case of brief quotations embodied in critical reviews and certain other noncommercial uses permitted by copyright law.

Print ISBN: 978-1-64649-130-8
Ebook ISBN: 978-1-64649-131-5

This book is dedicated to the millions of adults
who give care every day and night
to those whose health is in decline.

Metta to Caregivers

The light inside of me shines
I respect and honor the light within you
May all beings everywhere know their own light
May all beings everywhere live in peace

Contents

Introduction

I am a reluctant caregiver. Thirteen years ago, my mother's brain attacked itself and she suffered a stroke. It was the first stroke in our family. One visit, one errand, one meal at a time, I began to give care. Without asking my permission, with no review of qualifications to determine if I had the skills, the knowledge, or the patience to do any caring, my universe shifted. Since that sunny day in June, I have made my way to here one minute at a time. She died six years ago. My father is still here, and I give care. Every day I glide, slip, trip, and stomp along this long and uneven caregiver path.

Several years after my mother's stroke, I dragged my feet and the rest of my body to a yoga class. A bum right shoulder was still stiff, and my insurance company had sent notification that all approved sessions for physical therapy had run out. I was in search of pain relief. That one hour of yoga, sitting and moving slowly on a borrowed brown mat, felt like an extended vacation. It was nothing like I had imagined. There was no chanting, no thick fog of incense, and best of all, no chatting. No one there knew a thing about my crazy caregiving life. No one needed anything from me. No one expected anything from me. No one asked me to do anything. Had I chosen to sit still in one place or reclined on the floor in silence, no one would have commented or cared. I had stumbled upon a place to be with myself in silence and at peace. The pain in my shoulder gradually went away, but week after week I continued to chisel out that one hour for yoga.

Months passed in this routine. Naturally curious, I wondered about the origins and evolution of yoga—where it came from, its purpose, and why its popularity changes from decade to decade. Link-by-link, book-by-book, I read about ancient yogic texts, the evolution of various spiritual traditions and world religions like Hinduism, Taoism, Christianity, and Judaism. Turning the pages in a book about Buddhist traditions, my eyes rested on a passage about transforming suffering into peace, joy, and ease. I discovered the *Brahmaviharas* (brah-mah-vee-Hah-raz).

What this book is about

The Four *Brahmaviharas*, sometimes called the Four Immeasurables are: *metta* (lovingkindness), *karuna* (compassion), *mudita* (joy), and *upekkha* (even-mindedness). These four virtues are already part of me, part of you, and every person. We live them, reflect on them, and hope for more of them. They are called immeasurable because the amount of ease and peace they offer is unique to each person and cannot be measured. My exploration to discover more peace and joy and ease by nurturing these virtues continues. It persists through the nonstop, ever-changing life I do my best to cope with day after day, year after year.

Once you are introduced to the four virtues, the only requirement to practice them is one simple breath. You do not need more time, more money, more things, more people, more skills, more anything. There is no list of positive habits you must adopt and there is no list of negative habits you must promise to give up. You have all you need to live a caregiver's life with less stress, less anxiety, and more happiness. This might sound too simple, not enough sacrifice demanded or rules to follow guaranteeing it will be worth the effort or that it will last. I had those same doubts. Then I began to put words to my breath.

Over time, putting words to breath becomes routine, a reflexive response to life. Lovingkindness, compassion, joy, and even-mindedness do not give you superpowers to predict or prevent what will happen. They do encourage an awareness of the present, a pause to remember that you are here giving care, and a reminder that you are doing the best you can.

How this book is arranged

Part One will introduce the *Brahmaviharas*. A chapter will describe the virtue and how it is practiced. The chapter that follows will illustrate a variety of ways to draw awareness to that *Brahmavihara* throughout your day along with caregiving scenarios where you might find it most helpful. Every chapter includes short phrases or affirmations that put words to breath for you to use or not use as you like. When you feel anxious or sad, when you feel satisfied or tired, take a breath and let it out. Notice the words that come into your mind. If they are meaningful to you, jot them down to read whenever you want.

Part Two includes chapters that look more closely at specific challenges for caregivers and how daily practice of the *Brahmaviharas* offers both guidance and ease as you navigate your own way in this life.

How to read this book

Begin your practice by reading the opening chapter about lovingkindness as a reminder of your value as a person on the challenging and changing path of caregiving. Once you become familiar with all four virtues, you will discover your words and breath move from one *Brahmavihara* to another with little effort.

The purpose for writing this book

I do not understand exactly how you feel at this moment, but I know that you do feel. I acknowledge the unpredictable and endless variety of thoughts and emotions that overflow your caregiver's mind and seep into your heart and body. My goal is to offer sincere support and perhaps a pause or two in your day of perpetual motion. I do not have the answers, but I will share what has helped me.

The role of caregiver for my mother and father was not part of my life plan. I never imagined it and never would have chosen it. Like your own, the path I carve remains unclear. I have questions and fears. I have happy days and sad days. I am grateful for each one. I am exhausted. I will keep trying. The *Brahmaviharas* guide me inward so I can be a better person outward.

May you be happy, safe, and well on your own journey toward peace.

~Patty Collamer

Part I

1 | Metta – Lovingkindness

A Morning Intention

May my life today be of some service to another
May my lack of skill in words and deed cause no harm to another
May my own heart, mind, and body be open to happiness
May I know my inner light

The *Brahmaviharas* (brah-ma-vee-Hah-raz), also called the Four Immeasurables, are *metta* (lovingkindness), *karuna* (compassion), *mudita* (joy), and *upekkha* (even-mindedness). These four personal virtues are already part of me, part of you, and everyone. We live them, reflect on them, and hope for more of them. They are called immeasurables because for every person putting them into practice, the ease from worry, fear, and suffering they offer cannot be measured. There is no promise of great riches or power when you practice the *Brahmaviharas*, and there is no punishment if you do not. A moment of curiosity and a breath is all you need.

What is metta?

Metta (Meh-tah) comes from the ancient Pali language and means lovingkindness. The word is often used today as a broad and comforting term to encourage us to care for one another with consideration and respect. Lovingkindness first emerges as a wish of goodwill toward yourself and toward others. Those wishes of happiness, of benevolence, and peace for others can be offered in your mind and heart as well as your actions. *Metta* then becomes a way of thinking and feeling as well as a way of acting toward yourself and others.

7

How to practice metta

The practice of *metta* begins with offering lovingkindness to yourself. For many, even imagining that you deserve to wish yourself happiness is a new or even awkward feeling. But it is essential that you do.

With practice, *metta* extends to someone you love, to someone you do not know well, to a person who has caused you harm, and to all beings everywhere. It is an offering, a wish, a reminder. This distinguishes *metta* from a prayer. A prayer expresses a desire to receive; *metta* expresses a desire to offer.

Every day you inhale and exhale over 20,000 times. Most of those thousands of breaths happen without notice. One cycle of inhalation and exhalation makes room for the next and the next. If you pay attention to one or two of those routine reflexive cycles, you will discover that in between every breath in and every breath out there is a space. A space available only to you. Lovingkindness begins there.

Wherever you are at this moment right now, take a breath in. At the top of that inhalation pause, blink, then let your breath out. At the bottom of that exhalation pause, blink, then inhale. That is your practice. One simple breath is all you need. Once a day, once an hour, once every minute, take in a breath and notice the pause. Driving to work, brushing your teeth, walking the dog, pouring a cup of coffee, making the bed, or waiting in a line, become aware of the pause.

Putting words to your breath

The discovery of that space between breaths draws your awareness to a single moment of life, your own life. Once you become aware of that space, you can fill it with *metta*. Simply put words at the top and words at the bottom of one cycle of breath. Choose any words that mean something to you. One or two words is all you need.

*Inhale **I am here***
*Exhale **I am doing my best***

Find that space, that brief pause between breaths, to send a few words of lovingkindness to yourself. Rest your attention on that moment when you are not reminding yourself of another failure or flaw. Breathe lovingkindness in, and breathe loving-kindness out. You are not taking something away from anyone else. You are not neglecting your responsibilities or shutting out reality. You continue to move, to work, to give care. In one breath you discover a space to find a little ease, a little peace.

Offer metta to yourself

In the time it takes for you to draw one breath in and let one breath out, try to count the number of thoughts, images, sensations, and emotions you experience. The ability you possess to sustain all that mental chatter at the same time you answer emails, carry on conversations, and organize new work projects is nothing short of awe-inspiring. Pausing at the top of a breath with a blink, you become aware of a single moment. Putting words to that inhalation fosters ease to interrupt that perpetual mental chatter. Pausing at the bottom of a breath with a blink, your shoulders relax. Putting words to that exhalation fills the space with an offer of peace to yourself. This is the practice of *metta*.

Caregivers struggle with thoughts about receiving loving-kindness. Even the suggestion presumes you are deserving of lovingkindness. Your days begin and end with giving. Real and imagined expectations for caregivers multiply in your mind. All day, all night, your internal dialogue includes critical comments filled with "should-haves." You avoid standing or sitting still for a moment for fear that next unexpected phone call or email will reveal you are unprepared or wrong, again.

Even if you admit that sending lovingkindness to yourself could result in something positive, receiving it appears available only to some—to those who have more time, more money, more pieces of matching furniture. Being kind to yourself might feel both unnatural, and undeserved.

*Inhale **I breathe in***
*Exhale **My shoulders relax***

For one breath in and one breath out, consider the possibility of liking yourself a little better, at least some of the time. Begin with lovingkindness. It is free to give and free to accept. It involves little social investment and no long-term commitment.

Offer metta to someone you love

With only a little practice, *metta* can extend to others. First, choose someone you love or have loved. That person may live close by or may be separated by time or distance. You might think of a close friend who moved away years ago. You might think of your child when they were young, sleeping safely tucked in bed. You might think of a grandmother or grandfather and the way they filled a room with laughter and love. If a person does not come to mind, you might remember a beloved pet you said goodbye to, or the pet who today assumes your lap was created exclusively and perpetually for them. With one breath in and one breath out, you offer *metta*.

*Inhale **May you find joy wherever you are***
*Exhale **I care so much for you***

Choose any words that mean something to you. Say those words along with your breath. That is all the time you need. Mowing the lawn, jogging, picking up towels, washing your hands—whatever activity you engage in, you can send *metta*. Inside that one cycle of breath you find space in the present to send wishes for a moment of calm, peace, and stillness to someone you love.

Offer metta to a person you see, but you do not know well

Caregiving responsibility shrinks the time you spend with close friends and family while new information and contacts that become part your life multiply by the day. Extending *metta* to a person you only see when arranging or giving care provides another way to grow your practice. The offer of lovingkindness to those you do not know well at all opens your heart and mind to give and receive more ease and calm.

The moment you become a caregiver, the number and variety of professionals, organizations, and businesses you interact with increases. Phone calls are made to strangers and questions you never imagined need to be asked. You exchange details about doctors' orders with clerks at the pharmacy and the medical supply store. You collect names, phone numbers, and business cards from bank tellers, barbers and hairstylists, lawyers, insurance agents, state and federal office personnel. These new names and faces are added to the growing list of health care providers now part of your life: the podiatrist, audiologist, physical therapist, ophthalmologist, hospitalist, charge nurse, ever-changing nursing aides, and dietician. You become familiar with maintenance and housekeeping staff. Many interactions with these contacts are momentary, some you meet with or speak to only once. Some become part of your life for a week, a month, or years. Some interactions are pleasant and comfortable, many are not. With one breath in and one breath out you send *metta*.

> Inhale ***I wish you smiles***
> Exhale ***You are doing so much***

You do not need to know a person to observe, listen, and understand they have worries and troubles of their own. Every person is different, but without exception everyone experiences pain and suffering. With one simple breath you offer loving-kindness.

Offer metta to someone who has hurt or wronged you

Practicing *metta* for yourself, a loved one, and someone you only see occasionally becomes routine. You take a breath in and pause; you let it out and pause. There is little to no interruption in routine. Some days you notice the number of breaths that include a pause increase. Maybe you discover some ease at the top or bottom of a breath. Sending a bit of lovingkindness out feels safe and compatible with many "do unto others" messages you learned as a child.

Every caregiver knows the pain of feeling hurt, betrayed, ostracized, even unworthy. The person responsible for causing harm to you could be someone who should love and care for you—a spouse, a mother or father, a sibling, another family member. The person who inflicted that hurt might be a coworker, a supervisor, or even a stranger. The hurt may have happened yesterday, last Thanksgiving, or fifty years ago. No amount of time or physical distance guarantees relief. *Metta* is a place to begin.

Even the tiny pause between breaths might feel uncomfortable. In a single instant your mind can flood with awful memories. Mental scenes are replayed with stunning detail and you experience the pain again and again. Your body responds with tightness and strain and you feel stuck there, anywhere but in the present. When that happens, return to your breath. Follow its coolness in through your nose then pause at the top and blink, pause at the bottom and blink.

> *Inhale **I know you suffer too***
> *Exhale **I wish you happiness***

Extending *metta* to someone who has wronged you is an ambitious challenge. After all, you still feel the sting of the hurt they caused. Sending wishes for lovingkindness, peace, and ease to come into their life may feel insincere or so obviously unfair. Sending *metta* to this person is not the same as forgiveness. The decision to forgive is not a prerequisite to sending lovingkindness to a difficult person in your life. But forgiveness can release some of the pain in your heart, serve as a reminder of your ability to change, and experience a greater sense of well-being. Putting words to breath does not erase or heal the wrongs that have been done, but you might find you are able let go of some pain or anger.

Offer *metta* to all living things

Of all the lovingkindness to send, this may become the most natural and most powerful part of your practice. Living things include all people everywhere, all animals, all plants, anything that is alive. Living things surround us; it only takes a breath to notice. When you drive on endless errands, jog-walk the dog through the rain, or force tulip bulbs into the cold October ground, you notice living things. Choose to offer loving-kindness to every living thing you appreciate already—to middle school teachers and their boundless patience, koala bears, tiny hummingbirds, to children everywhere. You can also extend lovingkindness to any living thing you want to appreciate more—trees in the forest, blue butterflies, your sister.

*Inhale **May all living things be well***
*Exhale **May all beings everywhere be happy***

Enlarging your *metta* practice to include all living things nurtures this virtue that is already part of you. You send wishes of happiness and wellness without expectation or demand that you receive anything in return. You might begin your practice sending a breath of lovingkindness to yourself. The practice extends outward to those you love, those you only know a little, even to those who have caused you to suffer, and to all living things everywhere. Pausing at the top and the bottom of a breath, you discover more and more moments to allow a little ease into your life.

*Inhale **I wish myself happy***
*Exhale **I send wishes to everyone***

My own words…

2 | Living Your Lovingkindness

Who deserves lovingkindness?

The intention to offer lovingkindness to yourself implies you are deserving enough to receive it. Some day you might engage in a detailed self-evaluation to discover if you are worthy, but most days even the idea is beyond a realistic use of time or energy. You plan, organize, deliver, and evaluate all the care you give. The word "self" prompts the mind to add the suffix "-ish" and take on a negative meaning, something to be avoided.

For more than a decade I read books and blogs, watched TED talks, television ads and eyed magazine covers promoting self-care. Well-meaning friends extolled the benefits whenever they noticed the crease between my brows deepen. "Take some time for yourself. You need it. Get a massage, go on a retreat. Just relax." After a silent scolding for showing any of my inside on my outside, I wanted to squeeze their throats for uttering clichés and scream, "WHO HAS TIME FOR THAT?" These two reasonable responses have never been acted out. First, because my arms are perpetually loaded with expandable tote bags that carry way too much, and second, my carefully cued upbringing: when you feel most uncomfortable, smile, and keep moving. I do not have the answer to a method of self-evaluation. Personally, I do not advocate the use of a mirror. There is a huge difference between how I stand in shock at my reflection in the mirror and how I imagine myself walking with stylish confidence in comfy yoga pants down the cereal aisle in the grocery store.

There also is a distinction between taking a closer look at yourself and squeezing yourself under a microscope. That level of analysis would hurt. On second thought, however, that may be what we need to do. Once dissection of the self takes place all the way to the molecular level, I expect to discover that you, I, and most every other person on the planet are pretty much the same. Of course, subtle genetic differences, combined with the world we find ourselves interpreting through our senses and intellect, contribute to the great diversity in life, but deep down, we are more alike than different.

For thousands of years, great thinkers described and investigated basic biological similarities in humans. For over a hundred fifty years, we have had the science to confirm these. Countless philosophies and religions provide explanations to our limitless desire to discover the meaning and purpose of life. One recurring theme is the concept of a light within: a part of every person deep inside. This light exists to guide us toward understanding, happiness, and peace. The words of Siddhartha Guatama, the founder of Buddhism, describe the existence of suffering in the world and explain that no person will escape suffering. I agree. But I have also known moments and days of joy, love, laughter, and adventure. I believe you and I are worthy to feel happy even when suffering and sadness are around us that we must care about and care for. You and I have a light inside. One breath takes us there. That is *metta*.

> Inhale *I have a light inside*
> Exhale *I smile on the outside*

Caregivers live the same numbers of hours in a day as everyone else. What we have no time for, is to *do* more. While our bodies walk, bend, reach, and become more and more tired, our minds continue to run a perpetual dialogue reviewing, evaluating, and predicting. Many thoughts are about the task at hand, whether routine or unexpected. Other thoughts lay out details of possibilities that may or may not happen in the future.

Attending to all these scenes leaves us anxious and fearful. *Metta* brings us back to the present.

> Inhale ***I am breathing in***
> Exhale ***I know I am here***

Given all your responsibilities, fewer and fewer moments in thought remind you of all you have done, all you have been in the past. A moment of memory without critical self-talk can provide support from within. Looking at a photograph flips your attention to another place and time. Just a glimpse and your senses engage. You smell the room, the day, the perfume. You hear the giggles and snorts, the tears, the yelling, the music. You feel the love, the rejection, the excitement of being in that place. You taste the Thanksgiving dinner, the Halloween candy, the grape juice that stained everything. You see another version of yourself. Today you think about, worry about, care about different things. But some things remain; you still have that light inside and you are worthy of *metta*.

> Inhale ***I was there***
> Exhale ***I made it here***

Find a photo and rest your eyes on the image for a moment. If you feel something you like, stay with it. If not, find another. You will be different in each one. Some may warm you like the afghan forever draped over the ugly couch. You may feel the urge to rip one or more in half. You might find yourself in a belly laugh that unhinges your children at the sight and sound. A simple photo, whether on your phone, your computer, or in the drawer you always intend to organize, is a way of finding a bit of yourself—a moment to see you have changed, that so much has changed. Recognize and appreciate you are different today, without judging if you are better or worse. You have lived days and breathed life for yourself and for others.

*Inhale **I have done so much***
*Exhale **I am able to do so much***

Offer metta to yourself

Despite our pursuit of the culturally approved goal to be more independent than ever, we did not get to the place we are today completely by ourselves. There have been days or years when someone else made sure we had what we needed to make it to the next sunrise. They may not have wanted the job or have accomplished anything beyond that or even demonstrated what we could imagine to be anything close to love, but someone was there, a caregiver.

Lovingkindness, *metta,* is now part of your internal dialogue. The word pops into your mind unannounced and you let it rest there for a breath or two. Maybe you are curious and begin to put a few words to your inhale and a few words to your exhale, words you are not even sure you believe, and you say them anyway. All these thoughts are important and meaningful. All are *metta.* The benefit of the practice is that in doing so you open a place for calm in your body, a moment of stillness in your mind, and peace in your spirit. It takes nothing from you. It is not exhausting. You can make it hard, the same way you can make washing the dishes hard. You might choose to make offering lovingkindness a dramatic production, one more thing you must do before you get to the next hard important thing on your list. When the mental dialogue drags you forward and backward in time, save one breath in and one breath out for *metta.*

*Inhale **I breathe into this room***
*Exhale **I am doing what I need to do now***

Offer metta to someone you love

Lovingkindness will spread to include others. You do not need to feel you have mastered sending *metta* to yourself before offering it to someone you have deep, kind, or loving feelings for. They might live close by and you see them often, or they might be separated from you by time and distance. I often think of my best best BEST friend when I was eleven. We spent so much time together our middle school pictures reveal we had begun to look more and more like twins: same hair, same clothes, same necklaces. Activities, interests, college, and life eventually separated us. I do not know anything about her today, but I wish her happiness. I send *metta*.

> *Inhale **May you be happy***
> *Exhale **May you know peace***

You may choose to send lovingkindness to a person you love or a person around whom you feel at ease. Perhaps you wish happiness for a new friend you have made and want to spend more time with. A caregiver's circle of close friends shrinks rather than expands. The resources needed to arrange and spend time with others seem unavailable. You see fewer friends for social catchups over coffee or a glass of wine. You turn down invitations to parties. You send a spouse or sibling ahead to represent the family with a promise to be there later. When later comes you have no energy left to lift the sides of your mouth let alone formulate a string of interesting, witty, or kind words to share. Once you miss an occasion or two you learn the world continues to turn without you there. Declining the next invitation becomes more acceptable, even routine. Distance between even the closest of friends grows. A wish of lovingkindness keeps you connected.

Sending *metta* to a loved one stirs up memories. Love is never simple. Love does not always mean comfortable and happy.

Some days your thoughts might never conjure an image of a person to whom you feel like sending *metta*. That is life. That is caregiving. The next breath in makes room for a new thought. Let it come. Then breathe it out. That too is *metta*.

If you cannot think of a person to offer lovingkindness, or there are too many images dancing about in your mind, choose a pet or other animal you have loved with your whole heart. The cat imprinting its body on your lap right now, or the pup resting nearby with occasional snores or sighs. This is love you feel. Send them *metta*.

*Inhale **May you be comfortable***
*Exhale **May you know you are truly loved***

Offer metta to someone you do not know

Caregivers move mindfully. Our minds are perpetually full. We humans have the super skill to act as if our mind and body operate separately. Caregivers become experts at moving slowly while our minds proceed at Indy car speeds. And all wearing a gentle smile on our face to avoid questions and pity glances from friends and strangers. You and I have no time for those.

Caregiving responsibilities might evolve gradually as the health of your care recipient declines and their needs increase. Caregiving responsibilities can begin suddenly with a fall, an emergency trip to the hospital, an MRI, or a routine checkup that turns your world upside down. Phone calls and emails are added to your daily to-do list. Then tack on errands to the pharmacy, medical supply store, lawyer's office, and the bank. At each stop there are new faces, new voices, new names, new phone numbers and emails to remember. These are people you do not know well but you may see them every day or every month. You can send *metta*.

Some interactions are short, some longer. One day I spoke for ten minutes, an eternity in the middle of a caregiver's day, with a teller at my dad's bank about what actions I am expected to take after he dies. She is one of a few in town who have met and spoken with Dad. She listened to and answered each of my questions, then shared the sad news that her own father had just passed away. I listened. I looked closely at the face of grief and I sent *metta*. I knew nothing about her life except where she works. She is a person, and we all experience sadness and pain. I wished her wellness and happiness in life, especially on that day when she wondered if she would ever be well or happy again.

Think for a breath or two about those you saw briefly today. The barber, the optometrist, the audiologist, the cashier at the grocery store. They may remember you or not. But somehow, they are on this journey with you.

Inhale **You have helped me today**
Exhale **May you be happy**

One breath of *metta*, of wishing happiness to those in life who you would never know if not for caregiving. When someone acts with kindness, with consideration, notice. Be aware of how you feel, how grateful you are to receive, and send them *metta*. When someone acts rudely, there is no need to take offense. Some have their own health problems we cannot see. Some hate their jobs and it shows. Most people never imagine they will be in the role of caregiver, ever. Most will never know you or the persons for whom you care every day, but they have helped you to help them. For that, offer *metta*.

Offer metta to someone who hurt you

The practice of sending lovingkindness establishes a pattern of response in your caregiving world. *Metta* opens you up to quick reminders that you are still here. While no one fully recognizes or appreciates that, you do. Teaching the practice and reward of sending lovingkindness, the Buddha felt it too important to leave out sending those thoughts and wishes to someone who left you feeling hurt, betrayed, ostracized, or unworthy.

A vivid image of a person like this might crash into the screen behind your eyes. You picture details and you feel the pain happening again and again. Those details sometimes take up permanent residence in your mind and body. You can squash them to the corners of your memory or press them deep into your heart. They are all a breath away. This person may have hurt you decades ago on the playground, in between classes, on the orchestra trip, the team bus, church camp, or your office. The person treated you horribly or maybe continues to dole out jabs at your heart and mind. Your body forms knots that cinch your insides at the same time your outsides display no hint of that pain. Even to that person, you can send *metta*.

*Inhale **May you be well***
*Exhale **May your worries be few***

A person who has wronged you might be a family member. This person may not approve of how you have lived your life and now disagrees with how you are giving care to others. You are here doing the day-to-day work. Your sister, brother, or aunt might be miles and miles away, unable to be here even if there were an emergency. Regardless of your other day and night jobs, a caregiver's life comes with no description. You may be a doctor, a nurse, physical therapist, business owner or barista. The path you are on is unique. There is no list of required skills for the position. It was not solicited or offered, but it is yours. Separated by distance or a bumpy past—my polite word for family chaos—siblings and other relatives must work out a system of decision-making and communication without a roadmap to follow. The more family members involved, the more complicated this process becomes. And it constantly changes. And hurt happens.

The person who has caused you pain might be the person to whom you give care. This person may have spoken critical and hate-filled words years ago or yesterday morning. You continue to perform the tasks needed, often without help from anyone else. Baseline stress is above the clouds and memories become crystal clear as you replay them one at a time, over and over. Looking ahead seems pointless. There seems to be no end to the present. You question your ability, your purpose, even the point of all this. Take a breath in and pause. Let the breath out and pause.

*Inhale **I breathe in hurt***
*Exhale **I breathe out peace***

To offer *metta* to one who has hurt you, it is helpful to first choose someone not so close as the person you are caring for, or a close family member, or close friend. To begin the practice, send lovingkindness to a person who hurt you long ago. You may have never told this person what their words or actions did to you, and still do. Picture them in your mind. Feel confidence knowing we all change, we all make mistakes, we all stumble on different paths.

Plenty of people have said and done things to hurt you. Some may have been unintended, others you have no doubt their intent to do harm was real. This person may never suffer for what they have done. They might never even recognize that harm was committed. A wish for lovingkindness will not remedy your hurt or fill you with pity for them. If you choose, that wish can offer space to begin forgiving. The offer of lovingkindness will not include your wish that they suffer the same pain they inflicted on you. Promoting more hurt and more sadness in the world will never encourage peace. For just a moment, put words to breath and send *metta*.

> *Inhale **May you know happiness***
> *Exhale **May you see beauty today***

Practicing this virtue might always be a challenge. Follow one breath in and one breath out. The space inside that breath can be uncomfortable. It is far easier to lock your thoughts in the past or cast them to the future than to stay still in the present. Let your mind open to the next thought that comes and breathe. Maybe you decide to forgive that person, maybe you do not. But you can send *metta*. For a caregiver, the here and now is hard. This is work. This is a practice.

Offer metta to all living things

The teachings of *metta* practice include the extension of lovingkindness to all sentient beings. Strictly used, this term includes those living things that are conscious of their own feelings and interpret their life through senses. That finite definition leaves out most of the wonderful, beautiful living things I appreciate in life. This is your practice, and mine. If you wish to send lovingkindness to the forests of the earth, to the darkest part of the ocean and to all living plants and creatures, do so.

Metta is a way to connect. Connection is what keeps us human. We see, hear, touch, taste, and smell our way through life. Understanding that every being, every part of our world has worth, we send lovingkindness to all. We share in this life.

> *Inhale **May all beings everywhere be well***
> *Exhale **May all beings everywhere know peace***

The beauty in this *metta* extends beyond our comprehension. I am unaware of most living things, but I accept they exist, and for that alone they are worth recognition and appreciation. For caregivers this is meaningful. One moment spent sending *metta* to yourself and to others is when you realize that while you feel isolated in the doing, the planning, the cleaning up, the remembering, and the forgetting, there are loved ones—children, parents, relatives, strangers all doing the same thing. They provide care whether they want to or not. You are not alone. When you are in the busy-ness of giving care, you have no time to network or time to share what goes right and what goes horribly wrong. Days fill up with activity and overflow with insecurity. You are not alone.

When you are most tired, the offer of lovingkindness connects you to others, to the other caregivers who live three doors down and thousands of miles away, giving care that is needed. To the trees needed to provide shade. To the soil and to the oceans needed to provide food. Every person, and every part of this life matters. One breath of lovingkindness can spread wishes to all living things everywhere. That is *metta*.

Inhale **May all beings have what they need**
Exhale **May all beings feel worthy**

Accept metta from others

Sending *metta* to yourself on those days when you find no words to write down on any gratitude list, when even more roadblocks have landed in your way, the prospect of progress is unimaginable. *Metta* begins with yourself, and if you cannot even send it inward, how are you to possibly believe there is lovingkindness in others? You can. Take a pause and notice your thoughts. They may be focused on one problem, one set of details, one set of circumstances that just cannot be overcome, solved, or organized. Then take a breath and let words come to mind naturally. Notice if those words serve to encourage or disparage you. Then consider the fact that right now there are millions of giving and caring human beings all over this earth. At the same moment you send *metta* out to all other beings, they send *metta* to you.

> *Inhale **I fill up with the kindness of others***
> *Exhale **I empty out thoughts I do not need***

Putting words to breath

With practice, *metta* becomes natural. It is what your body and mind and heart will do if left alone for a moment. Guided by breath and your thoughts put to a few words, *metta* happens. Lovingkindness is there with each inhale and each exhale. One pause between opens the opportunity to return to that inner light that is already part of who you are. That is where peace is found. That peace may only last a moment, but you know it is there.

> *Inhale **I am all I need to be***
> *Exhale **I am kind***

My own words...

3 | Karuna – Compassion

A Morning Intention

May my mind be free from self-criticism
May my body be free from anxiety
May all beings be free from ill-will toward themselves
May my words and actions bring peace to others

What is karuna?

Karuna (kah-Roo-nah) comes from the ancient Pali word for compassion. Like *metta*, this is not just a way of feeling, but a way of acting. Cultivating compassion engages your natural sense of curiosity. With compassion you act with a willingness to listen, to observe and to learn, and then to do what you can, when you can, to ease someone else's burden or pain.

Books and articles written about caregiving often use the word compassion interchangeably with words like empathy and sympathy. In your practice of the *Brahmaviharas*, it is useful to distinguish it clearly.

Empathy is the effort to relate to another person by imagining yourself in the same or similar circumstances as much as you can. In short, you put yourself in their shoes for a time and try to picture how you would feel in their place. Children are encouraged to develop empathy by pretending to be characters or animals and by watching a playmate's cues about how they are feeling. "Look at Ellie's face and see how sad she looks. How would you feel if you were Ellie?" Considering circumstances from another point of view is an important way to encourage meaningful personal connections and genuine caring for others.

Some people develop such a strong sense of empathy they start to take on someone else's living, literally. Sitting with a friend during another long afternoon of chemotherapy, observing the waves of nausea rise, fall, and finally hit, you ride along with them. You feel horrible, exhausted, and unable to form a complete thought of your own. You cannot sleep, waiting for the unimaginable to happen. You become their pain, their disease, their fear. This exaggerated sense of empathy blocks you from offering care. This is not compassion.

Sympathy is the understanding of other persons' feelings, what they are experiencing. You have sympathy for a person if you feel a shared understanding of what they are going through. For example, if anyone, even a stranger, shares a story of the loss of their dog you might feel intense sympathy. Vivid pictures of your dog long gone fly into you mind—their favorite toys, mud prints, food missing from the table, and velvety soft ears. Expressions of sympathy often come in written or spoken words. You say, "I'm sorry for you," because you understand this hurt, this loss. Sympathy is important, it connects us to others, but this is not compassion.

Compassion, *karuna*, is a way to know the suffering of another person and still be able to help. You understand and feel what they are going through without becoming their experience. You listen, you observe, and you connect. Committed to act on this understanding, you provide the care that may relieve some of their suffering. This is *karuna.* It is a challenge.

How to practice karuna

Like the other *Brahmaviharas, karuna* practice begins with a breath. Wherever you find yourself, breathe in, take a pause, blink, and breathe out. One breath is all you need.

*Inhale **I breathe in to nourish my body***
*Exhale **I breathe out self-judgment***

When you practice *karuna*, pay attention to that inner place where your mind, body, and heart listen to one another with respect rather than judgment, with anticipation rather than dread. Compassion is a virtue already part of who you are. Cultivating compassion fosters deeper self-awareness, and with practice, compassion invites a meaningful and rewarding connection with others. You see the look of sorrow or pain in the face of a friend or even a stranger and feel a longing to somehow help.

*Inhale **I know others have worries and pain***
*Exhale **I understand their worry and pain***

Karuna begins with a look at yourself. Recall examples of sympathy and empathy you have seen or have lived. Be the observer of yourself and notice the sensations in your body when you are faced with the worries and fear and panic that come with undefined responsibilities. Feeling sorry for yourself or feeling so anxious you become physically sick does not get a meal on the table or move the trash out to the curb. Drowning in a pool of worries for yourself or for others until you become who they are will not make the appointment with a physical therapist or find the dependent care tax form to file.

Compassion does not mean you take something from one person and give it to another. You send *karuna* because you are aware and understand that others suffer. Listen for and watch for where there is need. Recognize that need and act in a way to bring more peace—open a door, bring in the mail, retrieve a plate from the top shelf.

Putting words to breath

A first opportunity to cultivate *karuna* in yourself comes with the breath. Interrupt the chaos of your caregiving day with a pause. You know and live the uncertainty that every day brings, and you keep going. Put words to breath and offer *karuna*.

*Inhale **My mind and body are overloaded***
*Exhale **I choose to let some things go***

Consider again that we are more alike than we are different. Every person will suffer. Closing your heart to others to try and protect what energy and sanity you have left will not ease any suffering. You cannot escape every challenge or solve every problem, but you can wish compassion for another person. You can listen to others and to that voice inside your head. You do your best to understand. You do what you can to bring some relief. That could be the offer of a smile. Begin with the pause at the top of one breath.

*Inhale **I worry so much***
*Exhale **I will help if I can***

Offer karuna to yourself

There are moments, days and even longer when fulfilling all the roles of caregiver becomes too much. Exhaustion mixed with discouragement, with failure, with no control over anything secludes you in a place where you cannot bear to hear one more word of sympathy or see one more face covered in empathy.

*Inhale **I breathe in so many feelings at once***
*Exhale **Let feelings of peace rest at my heart***

Deciding to act in a way that extends peace to yourself is an invisible challenge for highly sensitive caregivers. You take on the emotions of others quickly and completely. There is room

34

in your life for only a few close friends because of the effects of this reflexive sensitivity on your body and mind. You cannot feel and hold that empathy for multiple friends experiencing crises at the same time. When you do, your health is compromised; you catch more colds, have persistent issues with digestion, and worry over chronic forgetfulness caused by sorting and storing the emotions of others. If you are that sensitive person, consider taking some breaths to accept that your ability and instinct to care for others is strong. A focus on *karuna* inserts the sincere desire to put those instincts into action.

*Inhale **I am holding tight to feelings***
*Exhale **I can relax my grip and let them slip away***

Begin with the intention to offer *karuna* to yourself. Your ability to observe, to feel, to experience all the good and the bad without becoming those experiences develops the skill to extend compassion to others.

Offer karuna to others

You observe suffering, change, and confusion in those you care for. You hear words expressed from a place of fear and frustration from family members and strangers. You listen carefully, you watch carefully but you remain the observer. If you become their confusion or their frustration, you will be unable to help. That is where you practice *karuna*. You are not detached or uncaring. On the contrary, you have the skill and desire to give care to another person because you are not overwhelmed or consumed by their suffering.

Find more moments in the day to extend your practice to the suffering of others. Without exception, every person has experienced or will experience suffering. You have no power to prevent this in your life or anyone's life. You do have a choice in the way you respond to suffering. Compassion is that commitment to act when you can, in whatever big or small way available to try and ease that suffering.

*Inhale **May my thoughts be clear***
*Exhale **May my words be kind***

Receiving compassion encourages you to develop more of your own. Just as you are a person who deserves *metta*, you deserve *karuna*. Continually busy with caring for others, your mind, body, and spirit become so boxed up you close off all outside interference with this mess of your life inside. Like you, others are living, learning, and growing. Someone you know, or even a person you barely know may extend compassion to you. Accept that.

One breath in and one breath out. That is where *karuna* begins. With practice, it expands inside and out. Allow some ease into your life and to the lives of those around you.

*Inhale **May I accept any ease offered***
*Exhale **May I act to bring ease to someone else***

My own words…

4 | Living Your Compassion

Who deserves compassion?

It takes small effort to know there is tremendous human need in our world. Some is in plain sight and requires time and money to bring relief. Some is unseen and mostly unnoticed. People do suffer. Much of our lives are exhausted in the attempt to avoid suffering. We ignore, repress, or redirect it below the surface of living. Caregivers know suffering up close with all senses engaged and use every capacity accessible to make the suffering stop. What changes in one person's life changes part of our life too.

Karuna is the practice that teaches us to experience the present moment, take in what is happening with all we are and all we know, and then act to offer some ease to another person. The challenge is to do all that without becoming the suffering we are trying to lessen or relieve. There are no shortcuts to accelerate the development of compassion in our lives. This is not the message we want to hear given the fact that we need answers now to help us through a day.

We live in a society that thrives on shorter and more concise lists to achieve longer and loftier goals. My eyes are super keen to read and reread lists of behaviors I should adopt to achieve success, happiness, and fulfillment. Magazine covers are plastered with their promises. "Give up Three Foods and Lose Ten Pounds this Week," "Organize Your Closets for Free in Eight Steps," and "Five Poems to Maximize Long-term Memory." Lists are everywhere and I read them all.

I expect today's lists are shorter because we know our time is shrinking. Few articles clutter the internet extolling the 122 steps to take for the next twenty years to reach financial security at retirement. I am closer and closer to the traditional retirement age and I am sure I do not have the kind of time, let alone the funds, to get beyond the first half-dozen steps. If the Bible were written today, the Big Ten would shrink to three: 1—Believe in God; 2—Don't take anything that doesn't belong to you; and 3—Don't act out of hatred to hurt any living thing. Sunday school lessons teach us if we carry through on the commandments, consistently and with good intentions, heaven will be our reward. Heaven, a place where we will be surrounded by every treasure imagined and unimagined for eternity. For many, those lessons provide purpose and meaning in this life and I would never discourage that. But my eyes remain wide and ready to spot the list of behaviors to adopt with happiness and contentment as the big prizes.

Even during my early school years at Sacred Heart, I had no recollection of associating heaven with happiness. Eternal life, yes. Instruction on right behaviors began with those carved in stone. I memorized the list before I was seven years old, along with the list of Seven Sacraments and the list of Seven Deadly Sins. I never felt more self-confident or relief in repeating them, even in chorus with others. No doubt this was because I failed so much at living them. Before I turned six, I scavenged through my mom's purse to steal smooth squares of Chiclet gum. Teenage years were fraught with more missteps, often with my besties as cohorts. Sinning runs in my family. Many times, one of my older brothers chauffeured my sister and me around town in his silver Ford Capri to fill the hour and ten minutes it would have taken to drive across town, attend mass, and cruise back into the driveway filled with the Holy Spirit and intentions of living better in the week ahead. Instead, I felt more guilt. I never disclosed these sins inside the confessional, or to my mother. I did, however, apologize to God in private. I am probably not as loved as a well-behaved, less sinful woman over sixty, but I know I could be worse. I remain humble and grateful for the second-grade lesson introducing Purgatory.

*Inhale **I am not perfect***
*Exhale **I am just fine***

Offer karuna to yourself

Caregivers continue to try after we fail. Much internal conversation with the volume dialed high blasts through our heads as we review and revise our own mental checklist looking for successes and failures. At some point we toss the list, give up, and move on. That is a space for *karuna*. Deep inside, you know what to do next. You will find the strength required and the way to get it done. No list involved. Your ability to listen, your ability to learn, and your decision to act is compassion.

When we fail to live up to our own expectations, it is impossible to stay focused in the present. The practice of *karuna* is one where we look inward to observe ourselves from the outside. We do not have to become our hurt, our doubt, our fear. Those are internal reactions to what is going on outside. Caregivers know they cannot anticipate what will happen in the next hour or the next week. Worry happens, our physical body responds, and our minds become singularly focused on how to survive the next change. Our ability to listen carefully to others, to sort through immediate needs, is clouded by uncertainty. Our ability to provide the care needed is severely diminished. *Karuna* leads you inward for a moment, to see your way out.

*Inhale **I breathe in this new change***
*Exhale **I breathe out my worry***

Whether alone in your caregiving responsibilities or you have help from others close by or far away, you will be frustrated, have questions, and feel you are operating without the tools to get the job done. We might get through a day narrowly focused on five steps ahead and feel some measure of confidence and control. When we sit down, however, the number of details missing, the foresight we lack about more real and potential problems to fix, take center stage in our minds. Our inner critic drones about what we do and how we do it. That mental conversation generalizes to include perceived judgments by a coworker, a friend, a brother or sister, and to anyone else who tries to help.

In my early years, we kids were encouraged to face challenges head on, figure out what needed to be done, and get it done. My parents did not sit up in the bleachers to observe our shortcomings. They were never that far away and always had a word or two, or a hundred, to rein in our bodies and minds and set them both to the task at hand. They were not there to provide answers for us as if handing out gifts Christmas morning. Their job was to slow us down and focus our energy to learn or create what we needed to do to face whatever was up to us at that moment. Whether I met failure or success, or anything in between, was up to me. I was fortunate to learn a lot about success but missed out on the parts about how to fail. In caregiving, I continue to rely on those lessons. When I reach a goal, I move to the next. When I fail, I melt into a puddle of self-doubt. I can stay there for days. Attention to one breath gives me a moment to listen to myself, to understand myself. One breath includes the pause I need to decide what to do in the next moment.

Whatever feelings occupy you today, acknowledge them. Do not wait until they compress and pressurize in your mind and your heart. The action of pausing at the top and bottom of a single breath opens space in that moment to begin again and create a new plan. That might include action to relieve some of your own pain, your own suffering. If you need help, ask for it. If you need to walk to a different room, do that. If going outside and looking up at the sky for three seconds would bring some relief, do that. This is not an act of selfishness, but an act of compassion. You recognize your needs, you understand them, and you do something to help.

With practice, the first reaction to what you might call failure is not self-deprecation, but to pause and let some fear go, to let some hurt go. Breathe in and breathe out again, at the first moment you feel that fear. Do not wait. Make no plans to revisit those feelings some hour or day or month ahead. Inside you know what you need; respond to that with breath. That is *karuna*.

> Inhale **I breathe in new energy**
> Exhale **I breathe out confusion**

Offer karuna to others

Karuna, compassion, includes the intent to act in order to ease the stress, the suffering of another person. There will never be too much compassion in our world. Close by or from a distance, caregivers live that intention every day.

You cannot always be with the person who needs compassion. This is not because you do not care, but because the demands on your time and energy prevent you. When you see or hear someone suffering and have an idea how to relieve it, you cannot always go to them or communicate your thoughts. Your phone rings, you have another emergency to attend to before the never-ending routine of caregiving moves on. That is the moment you breathe in and breathe out. Put words to breath. That is the action. That is enough. That is *karuna*.

> Inhale **May they find ease in their body**
> Exhale **May they think with clarity and purpose**

When someone needs emotional or practical support, they may not tell you. They may show need in other ways. A friend turns down an invitation, or two or three, they make excuses for missing get togethers or they decline opportunities to volunteer on projects they have initiated or cared for deeply. We are encouraged, sometimes directed, to manage our own affairs independently. Even the suggestion of help from you may be curtly dismissed. When this happens, persist at being curious. Observe changes in appearance and behavior, listen for words expressing hopelessness. Decide to act when you can, to do what you can. An offer of *karuna* with breath may be what happens in that moment.

Accept karuna from others

Compassion is a way we share reality, a way to establish and sustain human connection. Be ready to accept it whenever given. This too takes practice. Appreciate that the person who relieves some stress today by offering to pick up your daughter from soccer practice may not be able or willing to do that next week. The person who looks up information to find a discount on the purchase of safety bars needed in your home today may not be able to give their time ever again. They acted and you accepted. There is no need to keep track of *karuna*, no need to keep score. When you end a phone call or press send to an email, or walk through another doorway, pause for a breath to recognize it. You may decide to thank each person who helped you some day. For now, acknowledge and accept their act of compassion.

*Inhale **May they know they have helped me***
*Exhale **May they enjoy peace today***

Putting words to breath

Your inner light persists. It is where both lovingkindness and compassion reside. Engage with that lovingkindness and compassion and meet the opportunity to give and receive peace, to yourself and to all others. One breath takes you there. All you need is the pause at the top and the pause at the bottom. Then put words to that breath. That is *karuna*.

> *Inhale **I breathe in the warmth of my light***
> *Exhale **I breathe out warmth to others***

My own words...

5 | Mudita – Unselfish Joy

A Morning Intention

May I see all the colors in the world
May I be open to happiness
May my day include the simplicity of laughter
May all beings everywhere know they are worthy of joy

What is mudita?

Mudita (moo-Dee-ta) comes from the ancient Pali word for unselfish joy. Like *metta* and *karuna*, *mudita* is a way to become aware of and accept all your feelings and then act in ways that help yourself and others. All three virtues are already part of who you are. All three are in your vocabulary and in your experience. The practice of *mudita* increases the opportunity for you to feel joy in your own life and then offer to share it with others.

Cultivating this living practice of the *Brahmaviharas* is where those virtues become a way for you to ease some of the challenges, some of the suffering life will bring. Unlike lovingkindness and compassion, however, unselfish joy is more subjective. What you experience as joy is extremely personal. While sharing joy unselfishly is often observed between children without instruction or coaxing, for adults this practice might feel strained and unnatural. You see and hear far more jealousy, envy, and aggression than shared joy in the world.

How to practice mudita

To be kind, to act with compassion demonstrates you believe in the potential good in yourself and in others. To realize that good, you must be interested and willing to look for the good. This is where *mudita* begins. You know everyone experiences pain and suffering in their lives. The *Brahmaviharas* introduce a practice to guide you to a place in life with less tension, less worry, and more peace.

Life with little joy is isolating. The realities and stress of caregiving draw you away from engaging with others beyond simple courtesies. You do not have time to open up and share your feelings but instead focus on what is needed now and get ready for whatever might be needed tonight, tomorrow, or the next day. Your social and personal resources are depleted. Everything you have is directed toward making it through. No one knows the exact moment when the physical requirements for giving care will end. No one knows when the emotional requirements will end either. Creating and modifying boundaries is one way you attempt to conserve energy and protect yourself from more anxiety and pain. That is not wrong. That is reality. But those same boundaries discourage unselfish joy.

*Inhale **I breathe in and loosen**
Exhale **I breathe out to create space***

Mudita is in you and in the world. Whatever the source, when you feel joy recognize it, be grateful for it, and express it any way you want. When you see another person in a state of joy, invite it into your heart and mind and body, then share it with others. Joy spreads when shared. This is true not only for close friends and family members, but with strangers, coworkers, or neighbors you have little in common with, and even those we do not like at all.

Putting words to your breath

As you navigate in and out of days, you take for granted that how a person looks reflects their feelings. Of course, that assessment is wrong. It might be a physiological fact that emotions can be seen and felt in the same moment, but we humans have perfected the social façade. You may have even received explicit instructions early in life to hold your emotions on the inside: your face should appear unmoved by an embarrassing situation or you should smile when you are most sad. Setting out to pursue and experience joy seems risky. The practice begins with a breath.

*Inhale **I breathe into my heart***
*Exhale **My light still glows***

You know joy exists. You see it on other people's faces, and you hear it in their laughter. But sometimes joy feels as if it is meant for them and not for you. Sometimes seeing someone happy makes you feel they are sucking up more than their fair share. The more this person is joyful, the less there is leftover for you or anyone else standing in the joy splash zone. You turn away from their happy face or end the phone call quickly and close your mind. Memories push through your thoughts of days that held expectations of great joy only to end in more loss or failure. As these scenes collect, your body responds with lethargy, your heart begins to close, and sorting emotions brings your mind to a state of exhaustion. This is a moment to breathe, to practice *mudita*.

*Inhale **My eyes open wide***
*Exhale **Joy is in this world***

Offer mudita to yourself

Pain and suffering are part of life. So is joy. So is compassion. So is lovingkindness. Inside you are limitless possibilities to increase and expand these virtues. Despite the immense and endless responsibilities of caregiving, you have and will always have choices in the way you think, the way you feel, and how you act toward yourself and others.

There is no reason to wait in vague expectation for joy to come to you. There is no guarantee in hoping and praying that today what you have dreamed about and longed for will somehow become real. Caregivers understand more than others that no one has complete control over much of life. You live in a state of heightened awareness, anticipating more of what you cannot control, and act quickly in those situations when you have the resources to help.

It is possible to create opportunities to make room for more unselfish joy in your life. If you see or hear someone expressing joy, let that spill over into your mind and body and heart. A snort, a cough, and a squeak can make you chuckle and smile softly. The sound of a laugh can be contagious. It is safe and it is okay for you to laugh.

A breath of *metta* is a reminder of your inner light, the calm place of inner well-being. One simple breath accepts you there. When your *metta* practice extends to others, the time in between breaths opens space in your mind and in your heart to see outward with more acceptance and less anticipation. You do not know what is around the corner, but you know you have turned many corners in the past and you are still here. When you are in a place of greater suffering, when your mind fills with more questions than answers, with less help and understanding from others, offer *karuna*. Decide to act in some way to bring some ease to that suffering. Then think about sharing *mudita*.

Offer mudita to others

Like *metta* and *karuna*, the practice of *mudita* opens your mind to possibilities you had not considered. When shared with others, *mudita* provides some relief to a loved one, a stranger, or anyone who is open to receive joy. Each virtue naturally extends from yourself to others. There is no limit to the peace they offer. One breath in and one breath out. A few words that mean something to you. That is *mudita*. That is enough.

*Inhale **I invite joy for me***
*Exhale **I send joy to everyone***

My own words…

6 | Living Your Unselfish Joy

Who deserves mudita?

Joy, a word missing from my conversational vocabulary. It appears on countless book titles, magazine articles, and calendar pages. It is printed on coffee mugs, t-shirts, and tote bags. All the books published about happiness and joy make me anxious. I have read them all, some of them twice. I read Gretchen Rubin's *The Happiness Project* three times. Percolating all those practices of joy, of happy feelings and faces, I reached a decision: when I find nothing on the planet to smile about (even my fluffy cat hisses wildly at me without warning) I have the option to notice at least the outward appearance of someone else's joy.

For many of us, finding joy is a lifelong crusade. That may be mostly because the concept is completely subjective. From birth, we process all life experiences through our senses. Once we gain a bit of independence, social cues are taught, practiced, and revised. We learn the approval of a social behavior by doing that behavior. Nearly all our actions are affected by perpetual and complicated social learning. If we dwell on that, fatigue will set in. Most of this living happens with little or no attention. Much of what we do happens reflexively, allowing us to get done what we need to. Thank goodness.

*Inhale **I have walked so far***
*Exhale **I can be still***

Our ability and our desire to create room for joy is in part related to how much this kind of life celebration was part of our past. Some families just seem to share more joy than others. My best friend's father was a surgeon. They lived in a beautiful house and drove Mercedes and long station wagons. Riding in the back was like floating on a cruise ship. (My family proudly owned a faded red and white VW bus.) My friend and I walked the three blocks between our homes a million times. Whenever I stepped foot inside hers it was quiet, the drapes were drawn— the sign her father was home from the hospital and sleeping. We played Barbie dolls and practiced cartwheels in the massive, finished basement, all at a whisper. She had three sisters and a mom who was always there. We had fun, everyone was pleasant and polite, but I do not remember a moment of un-shushed laughter or what I would call joy.

That mellow house was not unhappy, just quiet, and sometimes felt sad. In contrast, my household was never quiet. It was not exactly joy-filled, but loud with emotions for sure. There were five of us kids and a congregation of recruits from all distances allowed to travel by bicycle. My mother was stationed at the kitchen sink tracking all troop movements. She guarded the family food supply and kept the bathroom closet stockpiled with iodine, Bactine®, and Band-Aids® ready for the inevitable mishap. Sounds inside and outside included a lot of laughter. To me that was a place where joy began.

Offer mudita to yourself

Giving care to another person is a serious endeavor. Life dares us to find a speck of humor let alone joy in all the decline, all the uncontrolled craziness on our way to what will someday come to a certain end. Deep down inside, your light could use a bit of joy every day. That might begin with a chuckle. That can begin with a smile. If you see no joy in your own life, look for it outside.

Joy is what you feel it is. Joy is a split second, a breath, where your mind, body, and spirit crash into each other and the result is good, warm, silly, and safe. A caregiver's life is at the disposal of others. But your source of joy, where you see it, find it, and seek it out is yours alone.

*Inhale **Life is crowded***
*Exhale **I breathe in new space***

Discover joy in your routine. Most days I wake up and begin to give care. Starting with the cats, they get fresh water, dry food, and plenty of treats before sunrise. Family food prep follows with a check of ingredients and a retrieval of anything needed out of the freezer for later. A load of laundry started, I dress, drive to work, stand, teach, and sit for hours, then drive to my dad's, stopping along the way for incidental requests or refills. After that, I drive home to the care needed there. Routine. Every day this happens is my best day. MY BEST DAY.

In and out of that daily routine I give compliments to others, mostly to faces I do not know. After all, they might feel their day is much worse than my own, and they could be right. I do not know. Never assume their life is going so well. You never want others to assume they know all about your life and how your days are going. We are all complicated, but on most days, deep down inside, your light could use a bit of joy. If smiling at someone else's face is where you could feel an outward attempt to find it, do it. And be grateful for the chance.

*Inhale **There is hurt I cannot see***
*Exhale **I choose to be kind***

The concept of time for caregivers is one of all things that change. Months and years pass, unevenly marked by emergency room visits, career changes and worry lines. Finding joy slips to the bottom of any to-do list along with getting more sleep and taking a vacation. Joy seems like work and implies a prerequisite of more time and more energy.

For me, joy starts with the funny, a chuckle or a private smile behind the wheel of my car. That might not be considered exuberant joy, but on most days that is enough. I cannot remember the first time I laughed out loud at my caregiver life, but I know I did. Maybe after months of restless nights of non-sleep I slipped into a slap-happy mood and imagined my body taken over by an invisible mob of tickling hyenas. Whatever the cause, it happened. Once the inescapable guilt over that laughter subsided, I not only forgave myself, but left room in my heart, mind, and body for a chuckle whenever it naturally bubbled up and out.

*Inhale **I breathe in this life***
*Exhale **I breathe out a smile***

The non-routine of caregiving is never without the ridiculous. There are days you are surrounded by people who cannot see the obvious, do not listen, do not speak your language, let alone understand your more than reasonable and overly polite requests. Before you realize it, your habit of communicating with all health care providers begins with "I hate to bother you but," and "I am so sorry to ask one more question, but will there be someone here when..." More and more of your attention is wrapped in the attempt to be understood, by anyone, including the person you are giving the most care. More and more people respond to your words with faces exhibiting some state of personal bliss, and you begin again. Hours, days, and weeks pass when you replay conversations, then wonder if somehow in the business of giving care you have misplaced the skills to communicate effectively and efficiently along with your sanity. This is the moment to invite *mudita*.

*Inhale **I speak clearly***
*Exhale **I am kind with my words***

Then laugh because life is worthy of a laugh. Truly. You have not lost your memory, your good intentions, your heart, or your car keys forever. And you can smile. You can laugh. Let that laugh relax your face, your jaw, and your belly. You deserve those moments of joy.

Offer mudita to others

Eyes straight ahead to avoid distraction and the forgetfulness that accompanies it, caregivers walk quickly and with purpose. Consider extending a kind greeting, but recognize their minds are also full and they might be suffering. Understand the tight lips and fixed eyes that pass by with no response. Then imagine a scene of wonder or silliness. That special something that never fails to ease you into a smile. The practice of *mudita* creates a place and a moment for the funny, the happy, even the joy to slip into your day. When it does, practice sharing it with others.

Choose to be on the lookout for the possibility of the funny in life today and every day. Then do not hesitate to share it. The whole world could use something to smile about, to laugh about. It may not happen right in front of you, but instead come in the form of a flashback. I remember walking into my mother's room shortly after she had broken her hip in a bathroom fall. She immediately alerted me to "Watch out for the robin that just flew in. It's making a mess of everything!" Well-trained to respect every word my mother spoke, I looked around her small bedroom in the skilled care unit. Finding nothing, I replied, "Okay, will do." On my way out, my impromptu desk chat with the charge nurse enlightened me about a change in her medication and its side effects. My deepest concerns diminished but I could not get the scene out of my mind. I made it to the car, buckled the seatbelt, then busted into guttural laughs without care the whole drive home.

I shared that story with everyone I came within six feet of for days.

*Inhale **I am here in this moment***
*Exhale **Some of this is ridiculously funny***

Accept mudita from others

On days singularly focused on dealing with a lack of needed toiletry supplies, another appointment time to set up, and a curt response to a request for fresh water, our ears filter all words except the important. Many of us give care in the mornings before work, anxious to set things right for the day ahead, with guarantees of safety and the hope for pleasantness. After work we come back tired. We are wrung out from talking, solving problems, and discouraged by the unfinished projects we leave behind to tackle again the next day.

On the chance we hear laughter, our body, mind, and hearts respond with resentment. How dare another person have the nerve to laugh around me? They obviously have no understanding about how serious life is and how necessary it is to be aware and on guard for anything to happen. That is the moment to breathe in and breathe out. Hear that laughter. Consider that someone at work or at home might want to share a bit of their joy because they have missed your smile, they have missed your laugh. Their goal is not to take, but to share something silly, crazy, or amazing that happened.

*Inhale **I hear laughter***
*Exhale **I let it fill me up***

There is happiness in this world. It is not everywhere all the time. If a person shares some with you, join in, keep it tucked away for later, be grateful for it. With practice, you will be ready for it. We do not know when it will be offered again.

Putting words to breath

Mudita is joy, the kind of joy that is shared, contagious, and provides some ease to anyone around. You can choose to keep a place in your heart for the possibility. Take one breath. Send it deep into your belly and lighten up, literally. Use your breath to welcome joy inside to keep that inner light warm and bright. You need joy to grow, to live, to give care. Your breath is your own. The world will not stop spinning when you find joy. The phone will still buzz, beep, or quack. Men and women will still pull on their best sports jerseys for Sunday morning church services. Let people be who they are. Let the ridiculous in. Look for it, listen for it, joy is around you.

*Inhale **This is funny***
*Exhale **This is my joy***

One breath in and one breath out, joy begins there. Then send out and receive joy. It is contagious. We have all known or watched someone who seems able to turn any situation into something ridiculous or funny. We may even know details of their personal life that make us question their ability or their motives for inciting smiles and laughter. *Mudita* is unselfish, it is offered without expectation of anything in return. Whatever the source, accept it, experience it fully, and share it with others.

Giving care to others is demanding. It leaves us feeling isolated and serious as if we are living under a perpetual gray sky regardless of the weather. Be ready for that moment where you lift the corners of your mouth and experience ease. Put words to your breath. This is *mudita*.

*Inhale **I am so tired***
*Exhale **I can share a smile***

My own words...

7 | Upekkha – Even-mindedness

A Morning Intention

May I give thanks for the present moment
May I appreciate that all things change
May I give care without expecting praise or criticism
May all beings everywhere trust their inner light

What is Upekkha?

Upekkha (oo-Peh-ka) is the Pali word for even-mindedness. Of the four *Brahmaviharas*, it may be the most misinterpreted. The root word *upa* means "over" and *ekkha* means "look." The word is often taken literally to suggest a person overlook the present, concentrate on disengagement, and develop a supreme indifference to what happens to them and around them. It is almost as if you should pull back from life to not feel, not care, not be affected by what you experience today. That might tempt you toward momentary numbness, but a retreat from life will not bring you ease from suffering.

Upekkha reminds us we can be present to what is happening without overacting. Exploring the virtue of even-mindedness encourages you to see it all and feel it all. You learn to remain present but unattached to the good and the bad, ready to act from a place of knowledge and love. *Upekkha* may be the most challenging *Brahmavihara* to practice but it may show you the straightest path toward peace.

Upekkha, even-mindedness, begins the moment we breathe without judgment or attachment. In that moment, your awareness to what is happening expands. Without effort you acknowledge and accept all emotions and thoughts that come into your mind. There is no fear there, but rather, love, compassion, and unselfish joy. You use all the information you have and give all the care you are able to without being attached to a specific outcome or desire.

How to practice upekkha

Cultivating *upekkha* is encouraged when you understand and accept three things: you experience and interpret your own reality, there is a difference between your attachments and your likes, and all things change.

*Inhale **I breathe in here and now***
*Exhale **This is real***

You experience the world through your senses. One simple breath in and a breath out connects you to all of them in a moment. You see colors, shapes, beauty, and decay. You smell the place where you stand or sit or move. You hear outside your mind. You feel the clothes on your body, the air on your skin. You taste whatever lingers on your tongue and inside your cheeks. All of this exists in a single moment. There is no need to push it away, ignore it, or attempt to change any of it. It is there, you interpret, you feel, and you understand. This is your reality.

The practice of *upekkha* highlights our likes and our attachments. There is an important distinction to be made. Liking something is experienced in the moment, maybe a ray of sunshine that streams through your window in the middle of a cloudy day. You respond with a smile and gather hope for better hours and days ahead. Attachment is not the same. Attachment extends beyond a measure of time. It enters your body and mind, then stays there. It grips at your chest and shortens your breath. It is a mixture of happiness and fear. The energy spent in your effort to keep that attachment strong and forever is a barrier and keeps you from enjoying anything close to ease in your life.

Attachment can be to objects or behaviors or to ways of thinking that are fun, funny, healthy, and productive. You might be attached to objects, behaviors and ways of thinking that are fearful, hurtful, and sabotage all you have worked so hard to develop and nurture in yourself and in your life. *Upekkha* is the cultivation of a willingness to recognize when to hold onto and when to let go of attachments. This even-mindedness gathers lovingkindness, compassion, and joy together in one place. You experience it all. And you respond. There is no right or wrong way to feel, just notice. This moment will not last forever. But just one moment opens the opportunity for peace and more ease in your life.

*Inhale **I breathe in***
*Exhale **I let this moment go***

Caregivers know well that change comes, sometimes when you want it to, and oftentimes when you do not. You may not understand it all, but you know it. You observe it in the person or persons you care for. You observe it in yourself. You might make a plan to live an entire day ignoring change, but it remains persistent. Change can be a source of unimaginable pain and grief. Change is also a source of hope and joy. Regardless of your present reality, joy or loss, silliness or pain, all of it will change. You do not need to become attached to the good things that happen. They are part of your reality. You enjoy them, celebrate them, and share them. And they will change with every breath.

*Inhale **I breathe in this wonderful moment***
*Exhale **I understand this will change***

You do not need to become attached to your fear of uncertainty, of loss, of pain. They are part of your reality. In response, you feel the emotions and the physical sensations that restrict your breathing and speed up or slow down your pace throughout the day. Emotions and sensations will change with every breath.

*Inhale **I breathe in fear***
*Exhale **This will not last forever***

Putting words to breath

Begin your practice in a single moment. Focus on taking one breath in. Feel the air touch the tip of your nose. Let that breath out and notice your belly relax. Pause in the space between. Remind yourself that even when your perception of reality is cluttered with questions and anxieties, none of this reality will stay the same. Breathe it all in and let attachment to those feelings go. Draw in your next breath and move forward. In that pause between, notice peace.

Remind yourself that when reality is filled with smiles, happiness, and love, those moments will change too. Be grateful, remember, and let those feelings go. New moments of happiness, new moments of sadness will come. Regardless of your effort to plan and control, preserve and safeguard, change will still happen. *Upekkha* allows us to acknowledge and accept it all.

*Inhale **I am glad to have this moment***
*Exhale **I move onto the next***

Offer upekkha to yourself

Despite all attempts to control what happens to you and what happens to those you care for, you cannot. Illness, trauma, and decline happen. The fear that comes from that change is real. Improved health sometimes returns, needs increase or decrease, and so do your responsibilities. More change will come. All things, all people including yourself will change. You do not overlook reality, but you recognize it and continue to live it. Whatever feelings arise, move with them. They are your reality for now, and they will change. Without attachment, without judgment to the past, to the present, to what you long for in the days and months ahead, you can be right where you are. This is even-mindedness. You observe, you listen, you learn, and you do all you can. And that is enough.

*Inhale **I am exhausted***
*Exhale **I will not always be so tired***

Offer upekkha to others

Upekkha opens the way to gain perspective over what you experience through your senses and how you process those experiences in your mind and heart. Understanding that all things change, you are able to make plans without becoming attached to how those plans will turn out. When a day includes progress and happiness you are there to appreciate it and move to the next. When a day includes more illness and worry, you are there to appreciate it and move to the next.

The way you accept and move on is an example to those around you that life changes. You can be conscious of the pleasant memories and the unpleasant memories and still live in the present moment with even-mindedness. You look forward to and make plans and still live in the present moment. *Upekkha* is a practice that offers you peace.

*Inhale **I did my best***
*Exhale **I am open to something new***

My own words...

8 | Living Your Even-mindedness

Who deserves upekkha?

Reading about *upekkha* is reasonable; beginning to practice it teeters on the absurd. There are material things and situations and people in my life that I love and that make me happy. I never want to let them go, ever. There are material things and people and situations in my life that I work hard to avoid, to get rid of, and to ignore. To respond to everything that happens in life evenly, with the same amount of joy or sadness, makes no sense. My heart melts when I meet a kitten who needs a home. When the phone rings before 8:00 A.M. my body stiffens. I sweat frustration after asking a third time for a straw to feed my mother. When circumstances confront you, pressing an internal reset button in search of perspective without judgment or criticism is fantasy. Reality exists in your mind, in your body, and right before your eyes. You do not need a new book or another online discussion group to understand that. No combination of words can adequately communicate the cluster of thoughts spiraling through your head and down into every cell of your depleted body.

The concept of *upekkha* conjures an image of a bare-shouldered monk sitting cross-legged on a sage green hillside totally absorbed by the cloudless horizon. His peaceful face never commits to a smile or a frown. He remains completely still. I imagine the line of ants marching toward his bare ankle. He does not move. The ants reach their destination. His face, his body show no change. My eyes squeeze to stop the image.

Upekkha is the practice through which we learn to respond with an even mind to the good (clear sky) and the awful (ants).

That momentary image assures me I will never be a monk. I do not have time or the desire to sit still for very long. I doubt I could wear a face anyone would label serene. And while I have respect for all creatures on earth, I have a long list of those I do not ever want to touch my skin.

Responding to life with an even mind does not suggest we ignore or deny reality. Our caregiving life will include beauty and ugliness, joy and despair. *Upekkha* encourages us to experience all that happens without attachment to either what we hope and dream of or what we most fear. Reality is all we have in a moment. For one breath in and one breath out we learn to let reality be, without commentary or replay, without regret or excuse. Every person deserves *upekkha*.

*Inhale **I notice and I feel***
*Exhale **This moment is happening***

Offer upekkha to yourself

Discovering what you really like and what you are truly attached to is a curious and ongoing process. Even-mindedness teaches us to act and feel without clinging to either. To discover what I liked and what attachments blocked me from feelings of acceptance, grace, and hope, I did what I always do—I made a list. I started this one while on hold with the cable company. I wrote down everything I could think of that I liked in those minutes of captivity, then stuck it to the refrigerator with a magnet. Included on the list were a few material things: my mother's piano, photograph albums, my yoga mat, and my collection of books. It also included loved ones: Dad, husband, children and their spouses, my brothers and sister, and my dearest friend. I even scribbled the names of our cats that romp through the night and dogs we said goodbye to years ago.

Jot down your own list. Include anything that makes you happy or sad, angry or calm. It might be the mug you stuff pens in or the memory of your mother throwing her arms wide to hug you. Maybe you include your neighbor's scruffy dog that yaps nonstop every time you step out the back door or those two minutes of delicious silence holding a cup of coffee just before the day begins.

The practice of *upekkha* begins here. Glance at that list and separate those things and people you really like from those you are attached to. Images of people or things you like make you smile, chuckle, and quickly remind you of other places or people or things you like. You value each and they bring you happiness. You will feel terribly sad when you cannot use them, or they are no longer here.

Images of people or things you are attached to appear large and crystal clear in your mind. Any thought of leaving them, or them leaving you, freezes time with you stuck inside. The present is lost along with the perspective required to think clearly. Your body reacts with shorter breaths. A concoction of emotions whisks through your body until fear rises to the top. That is attachment. It discourages *upekkha*. The moment you feel your body and mind moving from the present to the darkness of fear, take a breath and pause. Let it out. One breath draws your body, mind, and heart together in a single place. Inside that pause is the moment where peace resides.

> *Inhale **My body and mind fill up with fear***
> *Exhale **I come back to now***

Return to your list and highlight the attachments. One at a time consider if the attachment to that thing, habit, or person is good for you physically and emotionally. Are you happy holding onto that attachment? Does the thought of it tense your shoulders toward your ears? Think of a person you are attached to and open your mouth slightly. Do you feel the release of a clenched jaw?

Caregivers need and deserve permission to feel. We need time and a safe place to let our emotions run out of our mouths, our bodies, and our minds. We also need a place to go where the action of moving and doing stop. This place already exists inside all of us. The journey there begins with a breath. Without the practice of seeking peace by looking inward, we begin to look for it outside ourselves. That is a source of attachments. You might stash chocolate bars deep in the refrigerator meat drawer and carefully break off just a section, or two, maybe three. The moment it melts on your tongue the universe slows and you gain superpowers. You know one piece of chocolate a day is not horrible. You also know that without mindful consideration, that delicious treat can lead to the bazillion-calorie venti coffee drink and the omnipresent pastry tray intended to induce the appearance of enthusiasm at morning meetings. You can paint the rest of the day's delicious mural.

*Inhale **I close my eyes***
*Exhale **I open my eyes***

Seek the relief present in a single breath. Consider yourself in the pause that is always there. Then choose to move in the direction that you believe in that moment is the best way forward on the path of even-mindedness. Be grateful for what you love without clinging to it. You can appreciate and still let go without fear, without guilt. That is *upekkha*. It is a practice.

Offer upekkha to others

Even-mindedness opens the possibility to live and love without discrimination or attachment. You do not attach yourself, your well-being, your mood to any one thing or any one person. You know when you feel happy and confident and you know those feelings will change. If something is wonderful today, celebrate. And know that will change.

When my father displays the first sign of a head cold, all my thoughts and emotions slide toward fear. Unable to project an hour, a day, a week ahead, I dig in and clear the way for improvement. I collect and dispense all remedies, call the doctor, decrease hours between my visits, and squeegee the apartment with disinfectant twice a day. I become attached to finding a solution, a cure, the fix. An unintended consequence of my short-term obsession with the cold is that I encourage more and more alarm in others. My father senses anxiety even when I hold my tongue. Anyone inside my house hears details of each day's progress. None of us feels anything like ease in our lives.

Practicing *upekkha* opens the opportunity for me to share even-mindedness with others. Rather than engaging in panicked behavior, I do everything to help without being attached to my father's cold. Despite my effort, I cannot see into the future. In the present, I see his discomfort and act to bring relief. Many days what happens is nothing like happiness. But there is certainty the circumstances will change. When I consider my options for steps to help him and then take all the action I know of to give that care, I am a living example of even-mindedness. I become a way of dealing with my reality for others to see.

*Inhale **I breathe into this moment***
*Exhale **I move into the next***

Responding to all things in the present moment and accepting they will all be gone feels like living a paradox. I am truly grateful my dad is here today. I know at some moment he will not be here. Even-mindedness helps me accept both without as much struggle to contain or avoid life. Putting words to breath, I use the pause in between and send *upekkha* to those around me.

Accept upekkha from others

A willingness to accept even-mindedness from others begins with observation. We process the present using our senses and then filter all that interpretation through memories of our past. This happens reflexively. When I am excited or panicked by circumstances, I expect others to mirror my emotions in their faces, their voices, and their body language. People who have cultivated even-mindedness irritate me when I am upset. My coping skills seem fixed, scripted. They appear able to cope with anything that comes along.

When I arrived home frustrated that another sweater was missing from my mother's wardrobe in skilled care, I expected everyone in my house to become just as frustrated as me. That response would validate my feelings and the mammoth significance I apparently assigned to the missing sweater. When that did not happen, I observed others respond to me with even-mindedness. This was an opportunity to accept *upekkha*.

Caregivers know when others are tired of our rollercoaster of emotions winding through the house. When I was pull-my-hair-out angry or wobbling on the edge of complete exhaustion, my son headed for his room. Hearing another blurt of anger, my daughter slammed her door. Even the dog disappeared to his favorite corner in the basement. Pots and pans communicated the bulk of my frustration.

*Inhale **No one understands this but me***
*Exhale **I let my feelings out***

Take a moment and consider their actions. Of course, my loved ones were not connected to my mother's sweater. She was not their mother, they did not drive there every day, they did not deal with perpetual changes in nursing care staff. They were not attached to the dream of creating a happy day and a perfect life for her. Rather than slipping into sadness with me, they offered a way to move forward with fewer emotional highs and lows. My daughter suggested I learn more about how the laundry is sent out and returned. My husband asked if more secure labels ironed or sewn into the clothing would help. You get the picture.

I am attracted to people who cultivate even-mindedness because it is reflected in the way they emotionally respond to life. They care deeply about their families, their friends, and their dreams. They share happiness as if they just discovered a twenty-dollar bill in an old coat pocket. And they exhibit no signs of devastation when things do not work out the way they planned. I learn from them. They stay curious. They listen and observe. They offer *upekkha*.

Putting words to breath

Upekkha means being aware of what is happening at the same time you are aware that all of it will change. Breath by breath we can let go of an internal grip to get things in their right place, their right time, their right relationship to everything and everyone else.

<blockquote>
Inhale I breathe into this moment
Exhale I breathe out control
</blockquote>

When I begin to let go of my attachment to controlling all things, fewer thoughts circle in self-evaluation and criticism. If you struggle to develop an ability to do all things perfectly at the perfect time, cultivating *upekkha* redirects your energy. Rather than evaluating the past and planning the future, your attention narrows onto what is happening at one moment in time, in one set of circumstances.

My *upekkha* practice was fostered by observing my mother. For many years her physical condition declined. Many of my days overflowed with change. At work I taught classes, chaired committees, wrote proposals, and advised young adults on career options. At home I attempted to help with physics homework, cooked new recipes, and took up running again. I was overscheduled, overtired, and overwhelmed. I discovered even-mindedness breath by breath. I felt no self-pity, and no anger.

*Inhale **I breathe in awareness***
*Exhale **I breathe out hesitation***

Like you, I never imagined life would include years of caregiving, but I gradually loosened my grip on preteen dreams of becoming a multi-lingual United Nations ambassador by day and a best-selling author of horse adventures by night. Letting go of attachment to how you want things to be opens your eyes to see life up close and experience the way it truly is. I still hate vacuuming cat hair off the stairs, but there on my knees I catch a momentary mental selfie of a sixty-something woman still moving and doing a lot. That is *upekkha*.

*Inhale **This is life right now***
*Exhale **An amazing adventure***

My own words...

9 | You Have All You Need

You have all you need to practice all four virtues

The *Brahmaviharas* give guidance to move through life as a caregiver finding a moment of openness and ease at the top and the bottom of any breath.

Metta is practical. Even when a driver cuts you off on the expressway because he or she thinks their entire life is more important than your own, you offer them a wish of lovingkindness, of *metta*.

*Inhale **May you find some peace in life***
*Exhale **May you get where you need to be safely***

Karuna leads to action. You observe, you listen, and you learn. You commit to acting in a way that brings ease to yourself and to others without being immersed in whatever emotions fill you up. You breathe with the intention to show compassion, and you do.

*Inhale **I see you are in need***
*Exhale **I am here to help***

Mudita begins with happiness, and happiness often starts with silliness. The practice opens your eyes to the ridiculous. There is plenty of that in your day. You discover laughter sparks the light inside even when your face and body lack the strength to move. Even that sensation can initiate a chuckle. Allowing the possibility for joy to bubble up, you share it with others, and it grows.

> *Inhale **I breathe in and shake my head***
> *Exhale **I breathe out the craziness***

Upekkha gives you permission to accept all of life. Every moment, every hour, every day, change happens. You can appreciate and let go. You can feel angry and let that go. You can feel sadness and let that go. You cultivate an even mind. There is less attachment and more acceptance.

> *Inhale **I will not always be here***
> *Exhale **I am glad to be here***

Remember these Four Immeasurables are already part of you. Your breath is simply a way to draw awareness back to that inner space of light where they rest. That light is always there. The awareness is a breath and a blink away. You have no obligation to practice any of the virtues. There are no required time restrictions, no special locations to get to, no rituals of public commitment. One day you put many words to many breaths. The next day you may not be aware you are breathing at all. Either way, you are still here. You give care regardless of your attention to actions, feelings, and thoughts. Know that kindness, compassion, unselfish joy, and even-mindedness rest inside and always will. When you have a breath, you have a moment, and you know they are there.

> *Inhale **I am aware of my inner light***
> *Exhale **My shoulders find their way down***

My own words...

Part II

10 | A Caregiver's Life

A Morning Intention

May I notice all sensations in my body
May I be open to all living and learning today
May I be kind in my thoughts and speech
May I be present in all my actions toward myself and others

Caregiving and stress

Caregiver stress is redundant. To perform all the tasks a caregiver must, you become expert at devising skills and strategies to cope with stress. Caregivers even put stress about stress on hold. A bold image of Scarlett O'Hara pops into mind. "I can't think about that right now. If I do, I'll go crazy. I'll think about that tomorrow." No one perceives the daily demands the same way you do. No one has the same responsibilities or is surrounded by the people who care, or appear to care, but do little or nothing to help you get things done. Horizontal and vertical lines on your face spotlight indisputable evidence of a thinking mind fixed on coping with stress, past, present, and future.

A practice of the Four Immeasurables creates opportunity to accept that stress will happen but with less need to try and exert control over your life. The practice allows you to insert a blink of mindfulness into the pause between breaths, the same breaths that prepare you, give you energy and the will to move forward one step at a time.

Stress and Sleep

Millions of words have been inked to extol the benefits of sleep. If you are a parent, you have chased after answers to sleep since your child was born. If you are the woman who carried the child, you had a head start, unable to find comfortable sleep on any side of the human body and called to the bathroom eight or nine times a night. You were in training for the life of a caregiver and sleep would never again be a light and funny topic to bring up in party conversation.

The amount and quality of your sleep has changed. After days, months, and years pass, you rationalize the entire process. Phrases like "Sleep is vastly over-rated," "I'm getting older," and "I just don't need as much anymore" slip out like addendums to the longer list of legitimized coping strategies. Repeating the phrases makes them more real and they take up residence in your identity.

The act of sleeping snatches time needed for your thinking, or at least you imagine that is the case. In the quiet of nighttime, your mind finally makes progress at working out the details of the daytime, uninterrupted by emails, text messages, phone calls, and other distractions people push into your life. In those quiet hours dedicated for sleep, you discover ways to schedule, to collect, and to organize information. You review the past day and look ahead to possibilities you can prepare for. In short, you have discovered another superpower—Midnight Mind. Your vision is crystal clear, and your thoughts are detailed, rational, downright brilliant. You have so much energy you hardly know where to begin. You have no clue where this vitality comes from and wonder why it will not be there when you need it tomorrow afternoon. Some caregivers keep a notebook of their Midnight Mind thoughts. Some order and reorder mental lists and eventually drift into a restful state with a brain full of confidence to use as tomorrow's fuel. Others will lie still, eyes wide, anxious for the morning alarm to sound so they can put all these plans into action.

Despite two bookshelves crammed with self-help books about rest, stress, and happiness, I have no answer to any question concerning sleep. Personal experiments conducted over time include various breathing techniques, yoga poses, melatonin, wine (both red and white), a gratitude journal, picture magazines replete with quick fixes, and reading John Bunyan's *Pilgrim's Progress* for the thousandth time. Each method lulled me to sleep at least once. Not one worked two nights in a row.

After admonishing yourself for not sleeping enough, let your thoughts return to *upekkha*, even-mindedness. Standing, sitting, or lying down, pause to practice. For that one moment at the top of a breath let go of any attachment to a quality or a quantity. Allow sleep to take up the time you have, and the time it will.

*Inhale **My body fills up***
*Exhale **My mind empties out***

Sleep will come. Honor research, then release any attachment to abide by a strict method to achieve the rest and rejuvenation science promises. A quick recall to earlier days serves as a reminder that indeed you have slept, and you have rested. Practice *upekkha* and know all things will change. Asleep or awake, you are giving care.

Stress and Food

What caregivers lack in the ability to manage hours of sleep in a day, they make up in determination to gain control in other areas. You must nourish your body, and you do. You know what nutritional food looks like. You know better than most the connection between nutrition and health. Indeed, some of the health problems you provide care for have a basis in the quality or quantity of foods consumed. You also live with a baseline level of stress for months at a time, higher than cirrus clouds. Throughout the daily routine you make deals with yourself: "I ate this cookie for breakfast, so I'll skip the toast. I'll grab food at Chick-fil-A since I won't have time to cook later. I signed up for a spin class tonight so this muffin will be gone way before supper. In fact, those calories may not be enough to get me through that intense workout, better have two." The number of mental minutes spent creating contracts over food intake is impressive. Some of it is necessary. Maybe you can let some of it go.

There is no one answer to the amount, to the variety, to the schedule of food intake. With lovingkindness you offer a breath of recognition and gratitude that you have food at all.

*Inhale **I notice this food***
*Exhale **I give thanks for this food***

Caregivers eat when there is time, and food is there. Maybe you eat when stress levels escalate to achieve the physical sensations of safety and comfort. Maybe you avoid food too long, as if the pain in your belly will keep you grateful, aware, and attentive. If you slide into that Thanksgiving feast comfort zone, you might miss something important and risk making a mistake. Like the moon, eating patterns wax and wane. But they continue. You are here and you try to do better. There is little good that comes from scolding yourself about what you have eaten already. There is little good that comes from promising food as a reward for achieving a goal or completing a worrisome task. A breath of even-mindedness clears space for a moment of letting go of that ledger of punishments and rewards. You are able to enjoy the food you need without being attached to it.

*Inhale **I ate that food***
*Exhale **I have the energy I need***

Buying and preparing food serves as a reminder you do have control over choices that make a difference today and in the future. You purchase what you know will nourish yourself and others. You spend time and care preparing that food and more time organizing and cleaning the countertops and equipment used to accomplish all that.

Consider moments when you look back on your day feeling as if what you ate defined you as a failure, inadequate to meet the tasks required. Compare that with the day you recall the spring salad you ate for lunch flavored with dressing you packed in your tote all while sitting next to your amazing coworker with the metabolism of a hummingbird slurping a giant bowl of potato chowder and gnawing a not-so-small hunk of sourdough bread. There are few things in life as unjust as the distribution of metabolic rates. That is the moment for *mudita*, unselfish joy. It is true that all human beings will have pain and fear in their lives. This moment enjoying a quick lunch with a friend does not have to include any of that.

*Inhale **Every body is different***
*Exhale **I take care of mine right now***

Notice opportunities in your day when you can make choices about what to eat and when for yourself and for others. Make the choice to put into your body what it needs, what it deserves, nothing more and nothing less. That will be enough.

Stress and Memory

You are a person and therefore you have forgotten things. Some more important than others, and some days and weeks more often than others. Even when you make lists, items written down rearrange themselves in order of priority constantly and you lose a detail, or two, or three. The stress of caregiving is punctuated by small and large upsets to whatever routine has been achieved for however long. You forget and feel as if you are losing it, whatever *it* is.

Take a breath and for that quick blink at the top remember what you are doing. You are responsible for you, entirely. You are responsible for others, some partially and another one or two or even three completely. You have meetings, memos, contracts, plans, and expertise to demonstrate. You have laundry, food, homework, supplies, dust, and dirt to manage. There is the dog that needs to be walked, and the litter boxes to be cleaned. You must produce the non-existent yellow shirt you just found out is required for the rainbow assembly at school tomorrow. Why no one stares in awe and praises you nonstop is one of the great mysteries of time. Repeating reminders aloud at various volumes, "What would you do without me?" and "You don't appreciate all I do for you," and "How will you manage when you are on your own?" changes nothing. Only you value the truly magical talent to put your fingers on the smallest misplaced item since god-knows-when in less than 20 seconds. Only you appreciate the frustration of accomplishing so much and then forgetting to take your dad to the barber at a time discussed and agreed upon three-plus hours ago. Go to that breath of *karuna* and send compassion to yourself.

*Inhale **I forgot***
*Exhale **I will remake plans***

Memory may be overrated. Doing is what counts the most. We all forget. Offer yourself some compassion. Understand the circumstances, learn something from them, then resolve to do your best the next step forward. That is a lot. That is enough. Chances are good that whatever you forgot can still be accomplished. The earth did not downshift in its rotation. The most important dates—doctor appointments, surgeries, out-of-town events—are recorded on multiple calendars, in all caps, possibly in multiple colors.

Other family members might be asked to engage their own memories. Your kids may have to remember to go home with a friend because you were called away to give more care. Your partner may have to remember to end their day early and get home to scavenge for food. Even with all this planning, it is possible a detail will be forgotten. With lovingkindness, reassure yourself this is not a worrisome sign. It happens because your head and your days are filled to the very top and something spilled out.

*Inhale **I breathe in this new moment***
*Exhale **I breathe out the past***

If the quantity of forgotten moments seems to increase, consider change. The brilliant and successful method you devised to organize time and energy changes along with everything else. In other words, take a moment of gratitude that your system worked so well, then plan for tomorrow. A bit of *upekkha*, even-mindedness, invites you to let go of any attachment to the calendar, the planner, the color-coded system that worked in the past, and let yourself create a modified way forward. All this without judging, without worry, because you know even that new system will change someday.

Stress and Life

Stress is a part of life. Caregivers have it, some hours more than others. You might look for outside help to reduce or get rid of it, and you might find that help. But the potential is always there for more. You know there is no one best diet and exercise regimen to follow. There is no one way to enjoy a full night of rest every night. There is no one supplement to take or trick to remembering all things. But you are still on the lookout for answers and fill yourself with "if-onlies"... "If only I could lose

10 pounds," "If only I could get some sleep," "If only I had remembered, none of this would have happened." Without those "if-onlies" you would be fixed. Life would coast at supersonic speed, but you would be able to handle it all. That is not reality.

You are immersed in a caregiver's life. You do not need to be fixed. You respond to what is real, moment by moment. No one else is living and breathing on your path. It feels lonely because in the beginning and in the end, there is you. Asking for help is okay. Crying is okay. Being angry is okay. So is laughing at the ridiculous. So is noticing one person being kind to another. Let the Four Immeasurables guide your thoughts and your emotions to that inner light of love that rests deep in your heart. Take one breath in and let one breath out. Feel the sensation of that love spread from your heart outward to every part of your body. Take another breath in. You are alive. No more effort is required.

*Inhale **My inner light shines***
*Exhale **I honor my light***

My own words…

11 | Anticipatory Grief

A Morning Intention

May I accept the energy this day brings
May I be aware and open to each moment
May my actions be from a place of kindness
May all beings everywhere know they are valued

Grief comes to all of us

Endings happen. Perpetually changing circumstances collide with our attempt to control the unpredictable future. A life you have known ends. The result is loss and the source of grief. The loss of an object, large or small, the loss of a pet whether they behaved well or poorly, the loss of a person whether you loved them or despised them—or more likely some emotion in between, the loss of an ability or a skill—you grieve them all.

No matter the circumstances that cause your grief and any suggested or prescribed set of emotional and physical responses to that grief, you chase after its understanding. You adapt to this ultimate life reality creatively, you ignore it, explain it, and imagine alternatives. For thousands of years belief systems have explained how to remove death from life. Rather than death as a fixed end, we rest in peace until a second coming, we live on in a different form, or we go to a place called heaven where our souls continue, happy, without pain, and understand all things. For children, the lesson of this prospect produces nightmares. Mostly due to the tandem teaching about the alternative, hell. That is compounded by the edict that either eternal resting place depends on personal behavior. Few if any come close to being perfect people. Looking beyond the inevitable ending of life on earth is a source of perpetual anxiety for many.

What is anticipatory grief?

Caregivers are different, even in the type of grief you live with and through. Caregivers experience anticipatory grief. You know the end will come. You also know that most of when and how it will come is beyond your control. Still, you keep doing, you keep caring. Day-by-day you observe and interpret loss through your senses. Some of that loss is visible. You see change in the physical appearance of the person to whom you give care. Their face has shifted in its subtle shades of pale. The bruise on the back of their left hand looks more green than purple today. You hear loss in their altered pace of speech. Simple words are pronounced three times before settling on one and their teeth clack whenever they chew. You smell loss. Their room circulates a personal odor cocktail made up of skin rash creams, toothpaste, institutional meals, clothes pressed against the same skin for hours, and the air freshener you plug in to cover all this. Some days the smell is so thick you can taste the loss as it happens. Every loose clasp of their hand, each embrace you feel no hug returned is evidence that less of your loved one is there. In between tasks, you imagine more loss tomorrow and the next day. Knowing that an end will come, these changes lead you to grieve the end of a life long before it ever happens.

Every occurrence you face in a day is filtered through past experiences with bits and pieces of predicted outcomes woven throughout. Feelings and facts are sorted, and the decision is made about whether to act and how. Those decisions can occur in a matter of seconds or they might remain undecided for years. The emotional expense dedicated to this process is unique and incalculable. You live through loss and anticipate more, never certain when it will come. With each day, the opportunity to practice the Four Immeasurables increases. One breath in and there is room for compassion, *karuna*. One breath out and there is space for even-mindedness, *upekkha*.

*Inhale **I notice change from yesterday***
*Exhale **I am still here***

Grieving the loss of memory

In addition to physical abilities, you might witness memory loss in the person you care for. There is no loss that compares with looking at the eyes of your loved one to discover they have misplaced who you are, who you have been, all they have done for you and all you are doing for them. In time, you may give care to a person who is more a stranger than a mother, a person who is more a younger sister than your aunt. But you are still here. They still matter, and so do you. This is the path you travel. Even-mindedness, *upekkha*, is a way to release your attachment to life as it was yesterday or fifty years ago. Your memories are preserved in photographs, safe inside your mind and in your heart. Share them or keep them with gratitude, every one of them. They are reminders that all things change. When a picture of the past comes into your mind, take a breath, and let it rest there. Allow the breath out to ease your attachment to that memory. Make room for the next.

*Inhale **I remember***
*Exhale **It has passed***

Stumbling blocks of living with anticipatory grief

In and out of days filled with people, routine tasks, and mini to catastrophic emergencies, details will be overlooked, blocked out, or forgotten. Mistakes will happen, more than once. Holding onto and reviewing them straps you on a cycle of nervous expectation that more will come. Anticipating

95

inevitable grief consumes even more of your energy when self-evaluation and self-judgment cloud every thought. Self-criticism plants a seed of regret. One item on your to-do list forgotten and you question your own sanity. The day you forgot to take the compression socks over, or the day you forgot that dose of the third part of their blood pressure medicine, or the favorite fleece blanket you swear you brought home to wash and now is nowhere to be found. Internal lectures on manners replay when you did not answer the phone after caller ID displayed who was ringing, again. What sort of person does that to their loved one? What kind of person would do that to someone who depends on them for so much? A mind filled with this chatter is just the place for regret to grow.

You and the person you care for have a history made up of weeks or decades. There is a shared past. Your memories of it are unique. No two people, even in one place at one time, will experience and interpret what happens the same way. Preserved, these memories drag you forward or shove you backward in time. They give comfort and inflict pain. They can induce terror. Words, smells, objects, even gestures can trigger one whether good or bad, kind or hurtful. In a moment, one sends you to a place where more memories collect. Recall the day you arrived to give care past the agreed upon time and were accused of only stopping over when it was convenient. That single comment hurled you back to when you were eight years old. Standing tall and feeling short, you were lectured about bad manners and your immature forgetful mind because you failed to call to let your mom or dad know where you were. This same person might be eager to remind you how other childhood characteristics seep through your personality even today. Despite the fact you have lived three quarters of your life as an adult, they continue to claim they know you better than anyone else. Yes, they know you. But they know you from the outside in and you know yourself from the inside out.

While you anticipate the end of their comments and remain aware that one day the end of their life will come, you try to silence or change them. Offer compassion, *karuna*, to yourself and to the person you care for. A breath in draws awareness to your source of light deep inside. It is always there. Compassion is the practice of understanding that this person does not know all you do and cannot feel what you feel. When they speak crossly, when they criticize, they show fear. They want to protect themselves from that fear. We all sometimes lash out at the people we care about the most. We desperately want them to know we are suffering in whatever way we express that feeling. When criticized, of course you feel anger or resentment. You feel small and weak. Waves of emotion continue to move in and out. The present moment is unclear. Reality pushes you forward, and the day ends with less confidence and more regret. Take a breath and let it out.

> *Inhale* **I hear those words again**
> *Exhale* **Those words are not me**

Practicing compassion allows you to observe their fear, their frustration without becoming those emotions. Do what you are capable of to practice empathy, but do not give over your mind and heart and all other resources expected or demanded. You cannot control their response to the care you give. You give care to ease. You act with compassion. Then offer that compassion to yourself. If you fill up with regret, find that space in your heart to forgive yourself, for what you have not done, and for what you have done. You give care. You are imperfect. This path of caregiving has never been traveled. You are doing the best you can. That is enough.

Living in anticipatory grief

Your life includes anticipatory grief. You adopt coping strategies to keep that anticipation from robbing you of the present. Some strategies are louder than others, and some are more self-destructive, but there is no reason to judge yourself, your actions, or your emotions.

Well-meaning friends and hundreds of authors reflexively respond to expressions of anticipatory grief by encouraging time away for yourself. But you know once the caregiver role is assumed or assigned, there is no more time left only for yourself. There are always at least two people to consider when making any decision about who is where and when. As dependency increases, long established boundaries between roles of parents, children, and friends blur or dissolve. There is no time off for good behavior, no promised perks for all the extra hours you put in. While you may find a way to get away from one day's routine, it is only in your physical body; your mind and heart never leave. Even the thought of an afternoon away conjures up a host of possible scenarios behind closed eyes: trips, falls, calls, your loved one sitting in the same chair in the same position when you return. The ease found in the pause between your breaths briefly serves as a reminder of the present, but offers the sustaining refuge no worldly comfort can.

Open yourself to receive lovingkindness, *metta*. The life that is happening belongs to you. You breathe in and out whether you realize it or not. Kindness draws you inward to your true self. Pause in one place with your thoughts and take a deep breath. Under stress, you take shallow breaths into your upper chest, almost as if deepening that breath will slow your thoughts. Lengthening one breath reveals the bonus of engaging more rational thoughts to order themselves. Consider the number of brilliant ideas or final solutions that have been discovered in the three minutes spent brushing your teeth. Occupied at the sink in that single activity, the body pays attention to breathing in and out to avoid choking. Shoulders relax a bit knowing you cannot wander too far. The mind opens just enough to offer a suggestion or a solution to something that has nagged you for the past month. This is *metta*. This is taking care of yourself with lovingkindness even when living in anticipation of the grief that will come. One breath and your practice continues.

*Inhale **May I be well***
*Exhale **May I find a way to get all this done***

My own words...

12 | Navigating an End

A Morning Intention

May I treat myself with kindness today
May I discover ways to help another person
May I be willing to accept help from others
May I breathe in life and love

Ends happen

When the person you give care to has been ill, there will be an end. Some day they will die. A part of your own life and your routine in living will be gone. They may have spiraled on a perpetual path of loss for days, months, or years. They may have suffered and endured agonizing pain. And when the end does happen you may be saturated in the double guilt of relief and self-doubt, questioning if you did enough.

Death and grief are two words discouraged as topics in casual conversation especially if you are experiencing them in real time. In fact, across the world the topic of death is taboo in many social settings. When death happens in our own culture, expectations dictate a highly individualized response to this profound loss, both externally and internally. Coping with death often includes several rituals where your most private thoughts and emotions are exposed. All public displays of emotion bring the potential for scrutiny. Like everyone, grievers avoid scrutiny whenever possible. You fix the I Am Fine mask on your face for show. Inside, the "what ifs" and "should haves" swirl in your mind. And without interruption, the never-ending list of life responsibilities continues to write itself.

Return to *metta* and send some gentle lovingkindness to yourself. Whatever you are doing, whatever your thoughts, pause at the top of a breath, blink, then let it out.

*Inhale **I know I did my best***
*Exhale **I release self-doubt***

Your thoughts about death

Regardless of your thoughts prior to this ending, your understanding of death will change. How you react and respond to others when they express sympathy will contribute to this change. A coworker offers words to connect with you, to support you. "This must be so difficult for you. I'm sure you miss them terribly." You suddenly realize that in the first days and months of loss you did not miss them at all. The sun stayed in the sky hours longer and there seemed to be no household chores left undone. One workday flowed into the next and no emails or phone calls were unanswered. Obedient to social rules you accept their sympathy with gracious gratitude and a smile. "Yes, I do, very much. Thank you." Then you hunt for a chair, sit down, and wonder what makes you so wrong about all of this.

Interpretation and response to death is largely a consequence of the culture in which you were raised. This includes all the experiences in your family, your community, any spiritual or religious traditions, and even government requirements of the state in which you live. Some of these are uniquely personal, others involve expectations for meeting deadlines, paying for arrangements, and even speaking in front of a group. In the early days of grief, you reflexively draw on memories for context and direction about how to act in the present. The days you are bombarded with imminent or impending changes you feel the physical and emotional energy drain. You may rely on a religious community that gives instructions for clear and unalterable ritualized responses after a death for guidance and comfort.

Offer *karuna* and engage with your compassion. In grief, streams of emotions flow faster and slower as they wind their way through your heart, mind, and body. The role of caregiver has already made you an expert at sorting through them all while still meeting the expectations of others. You may choose ways of coping with loss that bring temporary ease into the body, like using alcohol or other drugs that stimulate or relax. You may quickly increase and expand your responsibilities and time spent devoted to your job or to other family members. You may experience bursts of energy and make plans to start new projects or reset life goals. Or you may long to lie down and sleep for days.

You might pursue change or observe change without judgment. *Karuna* is that wish for yourself. Recognize any emotion, accept any thought without judgment. This is your loss. It is the greatest personal grief there is. There is no right and no wrong way to respond. You knew giving care depleted personal resources, but grief at the end seems to have wiped out any that might have been left. And you are still here. With one breath, you can offer compassion, understanding, and acceptance.

Inhale **Breathing in I feel angry**
Exhale **Breathing out I feel lost**

Put words to breath as often as you feel an emotion. Walking, driving, pulling weeds, or collecting the mail, the emotions will come. At the top of every breath is a moment to pause, a chance to send and receive compassion. You feel the way you do. You acknowledge that feeling with breath, then resolve to move forward to whatever is next. You are not your anger, but this is what you feel. You are not lost, but this is how you feel. *Karuna* creates the space for some ease in your life as you continue to navigate through this ending.

Be aware of the should-haves

Memories often collect, crowd their way into the present, and dominate your thoughts. Living with grief, it seems you have no time to fit today in between the past and the future. Having a sibling or a friend to help with practical tasks after a death is invaluable. There are forms to fill out, written plans filed years ago to retrieve, the funeral home to visit, an obituary to write, distribute, and pay for. Some tasks require close attention, some not as much.

A self-proclaimed Queen of List makers, I endured months of self-criticism for not writing detailed plans for the days and weeks after my mom died. My first and only priority was to lessen the responsibilities on my dad as quickly and as much as I could. For over a year I washed my face in should-haves. I should have known where to donate her clothes. I should have known about registering a death in the county. I should have had the obituary written and gathered the addresses of newspapers and organizations that should receive a copy. I should have known about changing bank signature cards and requesting multiple copies of her death certificate. After all, nearly eight years had passed since her stroke. What on earth had I been doing instead of those important things? My memories of the day-to-day, month-to-month, year-to-year routine of getting there, being there, and doing there evaporated and were replaced by the guilt of unpreparedness.

When a steady stream of should-haves moves quickly into your body, let your mind collect them in a pool. Then offer yourself the compassion of one who understands, because you do. Every day of giving care includes options. You focus on the present and determine the needs that require the most attention and the quickest action. As memories shuffle themselves in your mind, let them. They multiply and jumble and will not settle or sort themselves out. This is grief. A moment of compassion draws ease back into your body, mind, and heart.

Inhale ***My thoughts remind me of all I have done***
Exhale ***I am living now***

A moment of home

When a person is no longer here, past experiences assume critical importance. A colorful holiday scene comes into your mind, but you cannot remember whose house you were in. That missing detail becomes the underlying focus of an entire day. No matter what you are doing, part of your mind searches for that detail. Reflecting on the past occupies more of your mind for days and weeks than you ever imagined. After all, the past is where life felt ordered and predictable. Finding ease in those memories is not avoiding the present but serves as a reminder that you are here now, where life is not ordered and not predictable. Those memories can lead you to panic or produce random bouts of laughter. They are all there, and you breathe them in and breathe them out.

Inhale ***I fill up and remember***
Exhale ***I empty out with gratitude***

Moving and living in the present moment helps you feel grounded and connected to life and to others. So too does a memory of accomplishment, of satisfaction, of protection, of being home. The cold gray February morning after my mother died, I sat at the kitchen table in the dark drinking coffee. A sockless foot rested on some crumb the dog had missed and I whispered the habitual phrase, "You've got to get this floor washed." Holding that mug of warmth in my hands I stared into the darkness through the window and felt separate and safe from the day ahead. One more sip and my mind drifted to another early morning. It was summer, the sun was already warm, and I was seven. I stepped outside onto the back step in my baby doll pajamas and settled my bare feet on an odd-shaped piece of flagstone. My hair was wadded on my sleep-side and my stomach growled for Cheerios. The sky was canvassed in blue. Moments later, a black velvet-coated cat named Tinkerbell with an extra-long tail and a snow-white chin meandered up the stone path and passed under my knees. She paused, happy to accept the first cheek-scrunches of a new day. All my senses engaged in that memory as my mind, body, and spirit warmed. One breath took me there, to home. And I felt joy, even on the loneliest morning I had ever lived.

This is what *mudita* offers, a moment of unselfish joy. It is there and it is yours to return to in expected and unexpected moments. Life has changed. You still smile. You can laugh.

> Inhale *I am there*
> Exhale *I remember the happy*

Today, tomorrow and the next, every day is different

A phrase often echoes in the middle of chaotic change, "When one door closes, another opens." I had watched one door gradually close for years. And yet, when my mother took her last breath, it felt like a slam. All I wanted to do in that moment was to find the strength needed to pry it open. I had no desire, let alone energy, to look for any other door. Death was final. And I hated it.

For caregivers, the time and space within or outside yourself to sit with, process through, or even just feel is little to none. You may have anticipated this end for months or years, but no mental or emotional rehearsal is enough to prepare you for the next steps forward. Standing in my mother's room, my father gripped my arm, unable to move. My own shoes felt pressed into the floor. Ours eyes met, and in that fraction of a moment we recognized every part of our lives had changed. We took a breath together, and we moved.

The practice of *upekkha,* of even-mindedness, opens an alternative to the impending eruption of emotions you suppress. If your mind fixes on one memory that leaves you sad or one prediction that washes you in anxiety, just let that happen. Breath by breath you begin to recognize and accept that all things change, all things. Even your most vivid memories change with time. Let yourself revisit each one.

Upekkha encourages you to practice any ritual, adopt any coping strategy, and open your heart to any emotion you imagine might ease you to the next breath, to the next day. If one thought does not bring ease, let it go and make room for another. In that one breath, feel all the sensations in your body and become aware. Notice the warmth or the chill on your skin. Notice when your shoulders feel heavier or when the ache in your jaw reminds you it has been clenched.

*Inhale **That happened to me***
*Exhale **I feel tired***

With each new breath there will be another thought, another feeling. Balancing those between present and past, between happy and sad is not the goal. Allow just a moment for each thought in and let each thought go; that is where ease begins.

Once the inevitability of change filters your perceptions and begins to guide your response to life, thoughts arise without preconditions or self-criticisms attached to all the scenes replayed in your mind. *Upekkha* grows while the orderliness or disorganization of life moves you forward, not in a straight line, not on a clear and wide path, and sometimes in circles, but you keep moving. The good, the bad and the ridiculous will still be part of your days. Friends, relatives, and strangers will still make life more difficult or give just the help you need. Life pushes its way through even grief. You discover peace in your practice of *metta, karuna, mudita,* and *upekkha.* You will keep moving.

*Inhale **With every breath***
*Exhale **There is change in my life***

My own words...

13 | A Breath Forward

A Morning Intention

May I notice all of life around me
May I accept that all things change
May I care for myself
May I know peace

Find your walls, find your corners

I am grateful for corners. In fact, corners have become my primary source of hope. I have known children and adults who found their way around corners in life despite innumerable and powerful obstacles imposed by the will and control of others and their circumstances. This change did not happen as often as I hoped, but it showed me it is possible to turn a corner. After a death, imaginary walls appear tall and close. You might have rehearsed the moment of ultimate end a thousand times. To move forward, you search for a corner. Around that corner your feet step on a different path. You still find food to put into your body. You still find your way to the car and drive to the next destination. And you still care for yourself, your children, your partner, and your pets. And many of you have another person who continues to depend on your strength, your judgment, and your ability to help them. But around that corner, you realize all perceptions of time and space have qualitatively and quantitatively changed.

Uninterrupted responsibilities keep you moving forward, or at least sideways, at the same time your mind and heart want nothing more than to push time backward. For days, months, and then years, you replay those moments when the end came. Thoughts and emotions stab you and flood you in tears. They render your mind spacious but thoughtless. They cement your feet on the sidewalk and leave you paralyzed in a chair. The smallest task is trivial and irritating. Every part of your life is somehow changed. One simple breath gives you a moment to consider.

You have all you need to turn a corner. Return to those four virtues that remain forever inside yourself. It only takes one breath to get there. The *Brahmaviharas* will gently guide you toward a place of peace. There you discover ease for a single moment. And that is enough.

Metta – lovingkindness

Offer lovingkindness to yourself. Begin at the place where *metta* meets your pain. It does not have far to travel. After death, part of this practice includes more breaths of forgiveness than ever before. You no longer have tomorrow to improve on time management, to search for the better price on medical and personal supplies, to arrive earlier so you can visit longer. Tomorrow is changed.

*Inhale **I am sad***
*Exhale **I am still sad***

Invite lovingkindness to yourself. You have done so much. Some days with a kind touch and sometimes with a scream echoing inside the car, but you did it all. And now this part of your living has ended. Every day you learned, you gave, you changed. You will turn all the next corners in life with more skills and greater wisdom.

Your memories are not there to abduct your mind, but to sustain, strengthen, and guide you to every tomorrow. Memories preserve the excess, the deficiency, and every emotion from elation to despair. Some days they occupy your mind more than others. The "what-ifs" and "should-haves" cloud your eyes and you fail to see both the light within and the beauty of life as it changes around you. A breath serves as reminder of lovingkindness and eases your body through all of this living.

> Inhale *May I be well and happy*
> Exhale *May I live in peace*

Extend that lovingkindness to someone you love very much. Another memory or a photograph draws them into your heart. Whether they are still here, whether they have moved away or have died, offer *metta*. It takes one breath.

> Inhale *My heart has loved deeply*
> Exhale *I have been loved*

Perhaps you remember a close friend or a sibling you have not seen in years, a grandparent who smelled of peppermint and cheap perfume, an elderly neighbor who always let you win at checkers, or someone who knew you completely and introduced you to the peace discovered in love. Breathe in, pause, then blink. Put words to your breath. The lovingkindness that lifts your smile or lets tears fall is part of your living. It only expands when wished for others.

Next offer *metta* to someone you remember seeing after the person you have given care to has died. You may never have been introduced. The Sunday morning my mother died, her room was colorless and cluttered. I noticed the face of a young woman dressed head-to-toe in navy blue. Bright yellow logos and words were printed on her shirt front and back. She was an Emergency Medical Technician, a volunteer in our community. She had been called away from her family, her happiness, her sadness, to come and help my father and me cope with the present. Like all of us, she had cares, she suffered, and she still came. Wish this person *metta*. You have no control over how or when your offer of lovingkindness might reach them or how it will be perceived through their senses and life experiences. But you and I know there can never be enough lovingkindness in this world.

> Inhale **May she be well and happy**
> Exhale **May she live in peace**

Let your wishes of lovingkindness include someone who has caused you to hurt, to be frustrated or to be angry. Your chest tightens at the first thought of this person. When you needed them to be there, they were not. Their words compared and criticized. They were unfair and bitter. They showed fear. Take a breath in and offer *metta*. Every person suffers and every person can open their mind and heart to receive lovingkindness. You can send *metta*. It will never cause more harm, more hurt, or more anger. Sending lovingkindness to others increases your own.

> Inhale **May they be well and happy**
> Exhale **May they live in peace**

Days, months, and years pass after a death. The living goes on forever changed. You accomplish, you plan, you remember, you are wiser. When you experience this loss, this sadness, and this hurt, you know others are doing the same. People everywhere care for one another and still loss happens before their eyes. No life is without suffering. Uncertainty and fear make us feel alone and separate. Send *metta* to all people. You need no life details to appreciate that caregivers everywhere wake up early, go to bed late, and sleep little in between. Caregivers everywhere do all that is needed day after day in the best way they know how.

*Inhale **May all people be well and happy***
*Exhale **May all people find peace in their life***

Karuna - compassion

Even after death comes, tasks wait for your attention. Phone calls often come first. Physical distance between family members severely limits face-to-face communication so you turn to electronic connections. Sharing news of a death, even one you have mentally rehearsed for months, brings more stress. The response communicated back to you is unpredictable and beyond your control. There is nothing like a death to magnify family dynamics that have evolved over generations. Condolences from friends might seem awkward. They leak from mouths reflexively and revive emotions long ignored, denied, or covered up. You might respond to what you interpret to be careless comments with sharp words or mental promises of revenge. A moment of *karuna* draws you back to the present.

*Inhale **I cared through it all***
*Exhale **I am here through it all***

Part of your day, your week, and your life opens an awareness to learn. Every moment is an opportunity to experience and interpret life through all your senses. *Karuna* offers ease without criticism or judgment. You have been and still are the one doing. This life is uniquely your own. Compassion expands your heart to accept all life is right now rather than closing it off to avoid more pain. Emotions are felt but they do not define you. Breath by breath, open to each thought, each sensation in your body. One by one let a feeling settle, let it move, let it change. You have all you need to decide what to do to renew and bring peace. One breath in. Pause. One breath out.

*Inhale **I feel the swirl of emotions***
*Exhale **I choose to feel peace***

You are not responsible for what other people say and do. If they mean well, accept the expression of sympathy, of empathy. If they do not mean well, let their words fade and finally dissolve. You listen, you learn, and you act with care.

Mudita – unselfish joy

A benefit of knowing and practicing the Four Immeasurables is to experience their natural blending in expected and unexpected moments. Even moving through heavy air and surrounded by muted colors, grief catches us by surprise. A memory appears behind our eyes like a bright silver box wrapped in a deep red ribbon. Without effort, you smile. *Mudita* spreads from the top of your head to the tip of your toes. You feel joy in your body. Let it stay there for as long as you like.

> *Inhale **I remember every part of that moment***
> *Exhale **It was a wonderful moment***

If your memory is missing details, call someone who might know them. There is never enough joy in the world. When it moves into your heart and shows in your body, share it. Consider writing it down, retelling the story to a friend, or re-enacting the entire scene at the next family meal. Find the photograph that proves it happened. You were there. It was amazing, funny, ridiculous, warm, and safe. Years later, *mudita* is still a gift. With one breath you are there.

> *Inhale **I can't believe I remember***
> *Exhale **I am grateful to remember***

Upekkha – even-mindedness

Caregiving days consist of time divided between prioritized responsibilities and required tasks. Most days those are assigned without consultation, approval, or possessing the skills you need to get them done. The lack of control leaves you feeling uprooted and without confidence. Put words to breath and draw energy inward. In a moment you recognize where you are and discover your feet are indeed secured by gravity even if they are sore.

*Inhale **Yesterday was different***
*Exhale **Today I am changed***

Interactions with family, coworkers, and strangers exhaust your physical energy. New bits of information trickle in, new tasks that must be completed in order, your caregiving mind is saturated. You cannot make the most trivial decision without feeling anxious. Choosing which direction to pivot so you can exit a room produces mental chatter. You want to repeat what has worked in the past. You want to control what will work tomorrow. That attachment to control casts a thick shadow over any recognition of reason to apply in the present.

Scenes that play out in front of your eyes conflict with memories kept in your heart. Practicing *upekkha* enables you to release attachment to the way things were and to the way things should be this afternoon, tomorrow, or next year. Every experience is filtered through your senses and reasoning. Use those experiences to make decisions about what to do next. Change will continue to happen. It is not your job to know all things and control all things. You provide care today as you do every day. While there is breath, there is ease.

*Inhale **I do not know what will happen***
*Exhale **I have this one breath***

With practice, you recognize inevitable change in what you desire or cherish and even in what you want to avoid or deny. You live the next new reality without judgment or the intent to steal it away to keep forever. If the wonderful and the joyful in life change, so do the awful and the sad. Your heart might be bruised, empty, or broken. You may find little hope and less understanding of where the energy will come from that you need to keep trying. Putting words to breath welcomes you back to the present moment. One breath guides you inward and there you find light.

*Inhale **I breathe light into my mind and heart***
*Exhale **I breathe out the darkness***

All you need to move forward

The possibilities for choices you will make are unpredictable. So are the consequences of those choices. You make them the best way you know how, using all that you have. That is enough. Tomorrow you will know more, feel more, and give more. Practicing the Four Immeasurables will ease your way through anything that happens with less time spent on deliberation or self-criticism. Every thought that rests in your mind and every step you take today presents opportunities to move forward, to relieve suffering, and feel at ease.

*Inhale **I breathe in***
*Exhale **I let go***

My own words...

14 | Care Is Given, Care Is Received

May I receive kindness today
May my actions bring ease to another person's suffering
May my body fill up with joy and bubble out with laughter at least once
May I invite now and let go of then

We are born with few instincts and depend on the care of others to survive. Through observation, imitation, and instruction we learn the skills needed to take care of ourselves. The instinct to share those skills is evident long before any attempt is made to teach complicated concepts like empathy and social responsibility. Notice a toddler in the arms of an adult tenderly pat the back of the shoulder holding them safe. Without prompt, a young child breaks a cookie in two and offers part to a stuffed animal, another person, or a pet. A child receives care and gives care. The more we learn to do for ourselves, the more care we naturally offer to others.

The virtues of lovingkindness, compassion, unselfish joy, and even-mindedness exist inside you right now. Turning your mind, your body, your emotions to each virtue serves as a reminder that the opportunity to accept ease and to know peace begins with one simple breath. Offering those virtues to others opens you up to receive more. Picture that moment when you offered a smile to a passerby. The ideal world swirls in confusion when you discover the response to your kind gesture is not a smile, but an expression of suspicion or fear. You turn inward for one single breath and smile again. We remain human.

We all suffer, and we will all change. Give away what you have that eases another person's suffering and discover whatever comes. A big part of your life is giving. Let yourself receive.

Practicing the Four Immeasurables, the *Brahmaviharas*, is now part of how you care for yourself and for others. The practice does not require a schedule or any set length of time. The practice is not compulsory, but a possibility. Perhaps the four virtues become meaningful to you now, or some other time. Perhaps you share them with another person. When you breathe in and out, consider caregivers everywhere who are doing the same.

Inhale **Breathing in I receive**
Exhale **Breathing out I give**

Begin with yourself. At the end of a day, breathe in and out. Little by little, one simple breath at a time, let the peace from within give you rest. Another day is in the past and you have done the best you can. Tomorrow you will wake up and do your best again. If you can do something, anything, for someone to help them find their own peace in this life, you will do that. The true gift of learning, of loving, of breathing is to care for yourself and for others. All you are doing is enough.

My own words...

Acknowledgments

Thinking about those I want to thank, I realized I met all but one during the past decade full of changes in my life. I remember the kindness each has given and the many lessons they have taught me.

Thank you to my yoga teachers Misty Stillman and Holly Owens at Life in Balance Yoga for always making me feel I belong. And to Rachel and Ulysses Wilson at Om My Yoga Academy who live their yoga and teach that to others.

Thanks to all the yogis at LIBY studio, outside in the park, and on Zoom. You reflect the warm light of goodness that I often miss seeing in people.

I am especially grateful to the littlest yogis I have had the privilege to lead. I wish everyone could spend an hour a day with their positive spirits, insatiable curiosity, and contagious smiles. My world fills with hope whenever I am with them.

Deepest thanks to the accomplished authors who took so much time and consideration in reading my manuscript. Thanks to Dinty W. Moore whose book *The Mindful Writer* offers the best inspiration I know to begin every day at my desk.

I read Deborah Adele's book, *The Yamas and Niyamas: Exploring Yoga's Ethical Practice,* the first time during my yoga teacher training. I have read it many times since. It is a valuable gift to anyone seeking guidance for their lives.

To all those who read my manuscript and sent me comments and suggestions I am grateful:

Thank you, Lori Henry, for offering me opportunities to guide others. I am braver because of your friendship and wisdom.

I am grateful to Julia Hough for the depth of your insight into how to write in the best possible way to offer help to others.

To my Dhamma teacher John Mulligan for sharing your wisdom, your books, your time, and your boundless compassion. You light the way to take refuge.

Special thanks to my friend Debbie Freed. As a caregiver you know the importance of lovingkindness. Your beautiful smile and hopeful voice through every change you face encouraged me to write this book.

Thanks to Mary Pat Hough-Greene, you are the best friend I imagined my whole life. We live through the changes time drops on us by holding each other up every single day.

Loving thanks to my family for not abandoning me every time I declare my next hobby, project, dream, or scheme.

Thank you to Demi Stevens at Year of the Book Press who always asks me to do just more than I think I possibly can. I call myself a writer because of you.

Most of all, thank you, Dad. You make the sun rise and set every day. Thanks for sharing your stories, your limitless knowledge, your wit, and your love. I am the luckiest girl in the world.

About the Author

Patty Collamer is the author of *Grace on the Ledge,* a memoir of her childhood growing up in the '60s and later caring for her mother after a stroke, and *Grammy's Eyes*, a children's picture book about a family adapting to changes caused by a stroke. A retired teacher, she became a certified yoga instructor in 2017. She leads vinyasa practices and vipassana meditations. She and her husband love visiting their grown children on both coasts and are completely in love with their new granddaughter. They live near Gettysburg, Pennsylvania, with their jumbo-sized dog Riley and their mean cat Cricket.

www.ingramcontent.com/pod-product-compliance
Lightning Source LLC
LaVergne TN
LVHW041225080426
835508LV00011B/1077